W9-BUE-665

Starting Small Groups

BOOKS IN THE LEADERSHIP INSIGHT SERIES

Starting Small Groups: Building Communities That Matter
Jeffrey Arnold

Unlocking Church Doors: Ten Keys to Positive Change
Paul Mundey

Leading Your Ministry
Alan E. Nelson

Body Building: Creating a Ministry Team Through Spiritual Gifts
Brian Kelley Bauknight

The Pastor's Start-Up Manual: Beginning a New Pastorate
Robert H. Ramey, Jr.

Leadership Is the Key: Unlocking Your Ministry Effectiveness
Herb Miller

LEADERSHIP INSIGHT SERIES
LEADERSHIP INSIGHT SERIES
LEADERSHIP INSIGHT SERIES

Starting Small Groups

Building Communities That Matter

HERB MILLER, EDITOR

A moment of insight is worth a lifetime of experience

JEFFREY ARNOLD

Abingdon Press
Nashville

STARTING SMALL GROUPS:
BUILDING COMMUNITIES THAT MATTER

Copyright © 1997 by Abingdon Press

This book is printed on recycled, acid-free paper.

ISBN: 0-687-01856-0

Scripture quotations are taken from the *Holy Bible: New International Version* Copyright © 1973,
1978, 1984 by the International Bible Society. Used by permission of Zondervan Bible Publishers.

97 98 99 00 01 02 03 04 05 06—10 9 8 7 6 5 4 3 2 1

MANUFACTURED IN THE UNITED STATES OF AMERICA

To my wife, Karen, and my children,
Brett, Heather, and Hannah.
I never dreamed life could be this good.

Contents

Contents

PART THREE: IMPLEMENTING THE PLAN

FOREWORD

Small groups are much discussed by church leaders. Distinguished researchers such as George Gallup, Jr., George Barna, and Robert Wuthnow have found that small groups generate spiritual growth among Christians. Well-known pastors such as Dale Galloway, Michael Slaughter, and Bill Hybels have proved that small groups increase church vitality.

Why, then, do so few congregations involve more than 5 percent of their members in groups of ten to twelve persons that meet weekly or bimonthly for Bible study, prayer, and sharing? The answer is twofold: motivation and knowledge. Because they do not understand the value of small groups, some leaders lack the motivation to establish them. Other church leaders lack the know-how to establish and multiply small groups.

The strength of a congregation's small group ministry depends on multiple factors: (a) Whether the type of groups provided matches the needs of people in every adult age bracket in the congregation, (b) the quality of each group's leadership, (c) the quality of each group's interpersonal relationship atmosphere, (d) the congregation's written or unwritten expectations regarding whether members should be involved in a group of some type, (e) the effectiveness of the church's system for drawing new and present members into the groups, and (f) how hard the clergy and lay leaders work at getting church members involved in the various types of groups. If several of those factors are missing in a congregation, the number of people who report spiritual growth through small-group participation stays small. If most of those factors are present, many people find their spiritual growth enhanced through group participation.

Jeffrey Arnold addresses those and other small-group ministry development issues in practical ways that are usable in congregations of every size. His strategic planning procedures show leaders ways to accelerate from zero to sixty-five while minimizing accidents, driver fatigue, and back-seat-driver irritations.

After Jesus was crucified, two disciples on their way to Emmaus were talking about what had happened. "As they talked and discussed these things with each other, Jesus himself came up and walked along with them" (Luke 24:15). Since that day, millions of other disciples have found that when they come together and focus on spiritual matters the mind of Christ often joins them. When they come together regularly for Bible study, prayer, and sharing, Christ energizes their lives between the meetings. When that happens among numerous members in a congregation, vitality in all its ministries increases.

Arnold provides the organizational and leadership tools for leaders who wish to accomplish those ministry goals.

Herb Miller
Lubbock, Texas

INTRODUCTION

S mall groups produce multiple benefits. They can release the ministry of the laity, offer superior pastoral care, and better challenge people to be like Jesus Christ. Yet many churches run into roadblocks and encounter frustrations. Groups seem to easily become ingrown and directionless, while leaders run the gamut of personality and style. The problems and possibilities for small groups are complex.

Congregations who want to encourage small group ministry need to learn how to build on its strengths while negating its potential weaknesses. To accomplish this, you must carefully reflect on your past, present, and future small group involvement.

Most, if not all, churches, have some form of small groups. But does your congregation have a small group ministry? Are actual needs being met, are the groups successful, and do you know what "success" entails?

This book will help you tackle assumptions like "We already have small group ministry"; or "We tried small groups once, and they did not work for our church." By taking on assumptions and persistently asking deep, probing questions, you will construct a detailed plan of action. Your plan will more effectively ensure that ministry occurs at all levels of the small group structure.

After making a careful analysis of your current situation, you will prepare a plan. By implementing that plan—using standards and goals you develop for your unique situation—you will guide your church toward an exciting and comprehensive small group ministry.

Most leaders are acutely aware of the prime danger in self-studies and strategic planning: the tendency is to study carefully, and then do nothing.

Yet, few organizations accomplish great things without some homework. We expect generals to plan before battle, and corporate leaders to study every possible angle before introducing a new product. Likewise, church leaders who develop an effective small group ministry must have a plan.

This resource provides three tools for building and implementing that plan. (1) The main body of the book, filled with stories and examples, illustrates the planning process. (2) At the end of each chapter, questions are provided which enable you to develop your church's unique plan. (3) The appendix includes one church's strategy as a point of comparison.

The tools in these pages can be used in at least five different ways:

Option 1: Individual pastors or lay leaders. Study at your own pace, perhaps supplementing this information with some of the resources found in the appendix.

A pastor can then move in one of the three following directions:

- "Sell" the idea to church leaders and members, perhaps by preaching a sermon series that paves the way.
- Begin a "pilot" small group in the church using potential leaders. Eventually give them the completed plan so they can begin groups like those you design and lead.
- If you are leaving one church for another, send the small group strategy to the leaders of the new church so they can see how and why you will use small group ministry.

A lay person working alone will find it difficult to institute a church-wide strategy. However, he or she can study this resource to design one group. If the group succeeds, then it may multiply, beginning a small group movement. Most lay persons make better progress by getting a committee and/or a pastor excited about small groups, and proceeding to options two or three below.

Option 2: Committee within a church. You may choose to cover one chapter per month (among various time options), completing the plan within one year.

Option 3: Pastor and committee. You may choose to cover one chapter per month, completing the plan within one year (perhaps adding a retreat at the end). In this way, a solid core of individuals is involved in the planning process, and can work together during the selling and implementing stages.

Option 4: Group of pastors from different congregations. A pastor who participates in monthly clergy meetings might convince a group of pastors to dedicate a year of monthly meetings. The clergy act as coaches for one another, compare answers, and develop plans for diverse settings.

Option 5: Preparation + intensive planning retreat. Any of the above options is enhanced by tagging a planning retreat onto the end, perhaps in order to complete the final strategy document of chapter 11. If the committee/group meets for ten months and completes the first ten chapters, it can then meet for one, two, or three days and finish the strategy as part of chapter 11's work.

Forty years ago a revolution began in the church. Unlike other revolutions from two thousand years of church history, this one does not involve a theological misunderstanding or doctrinal dispute.

This quiet revolution has slowly built from the ground up into a crescendo that is more and more difficult to ignore. It has influenced every church's ministry in one way or another, and affected many people's lives. Damaged relationships have been repaired. Churches have been energized. People have come to faith in Jesus Christ.

What is this revolution? After centuries of institutionalization, the church is returning to the homes and lives of its people. It is drawing strength from its roots, *following in the footsteps of its Master,* who lived and walked among the people.

The agents of this change are *small groups,* although other titles are equally appropriate: K-groups, caring groups, sharing groups, Bible study groups, covenant groups, or cell groups. Small group ministry is sweeping the church and writing another chapter in its rich heritage.

By God's grace, and by applying God's wisdom, your congregation can benefit from and contribute to this revolution.

PART ONE
WHY HAVE A PLAN?

CHAPTER 1

SMALL GROUP BASICS

Ideas with great potential sometimes fail. Small groups are no exception. I know a man who sleeps each week during his small group meeting. One woman kills every group she joins. Another woman finds a way to divide her group through gossip. A church is splitting apart, and its groups are leading the way toward division. And many groups settle for a pseudo-intimacy that is more destructive than it is helpful.

Sociologist Robert Wuthnow of Princeton University, in partnership with the Gallup organization, has completed a significant study of small groups in American culture, entitled *Sharing the Journey*.[1] His conclusions illustrate both good and bad news. Some of the good news: About 45 percent of Americans are in some form of a small group, and many more indicate an interest in joining one or more groups. Of those people in groups, 60 percent are in church-related groups, and a large portion of the remaining 40 percent are studying spiritual issues. These statistics demonstrate that small groups are a powerful, significant force in American culture.

On the negative side we find several less quantifiable issues related to small groups. First is the fact that this strong movement toward small groups has not been able to stem America's cultural and relational breakdown. Then, group members often move freely from one group to another with no lasting commitment to a particular group, and many groups have a lowest-common-denominator theology that calls for no sacrifice or service on the part of their members.

Churches preparing to develop holistic small group ministry should prayerfully plan so that they can build on the strengths and bypass the weaknesses of these findings. This chapter is designed to present an overview of issues that leaders and planners must confront as they design a small group ministry.

Why Are Small Groups Important?

Small groups are valuable for *sociological, biblical,* and *theological reasons.*

Sociological Reasons: Small groups can help to address deep cultural and social needs in at least four ways: First, small groups provide a safe place where people can be heard. Second, small groups give our dysfunctional society a positive model for building healthy relationships, helping to strengthen the family and other interactions. Third, since people are known deeply in small group settings, they are prayed for, cared for, and challenged in a way no other church structure can offer. Finally, small groups can keep people on the cutting edge by constantly demanding more in the way of Christian discipleship.

In his best-seller *Dying for Change,*[2] Leith Anderson lists ten trends that affect Americans in every area of life, including their relationship with the church:

1. *Mobility*—This includes constant moves to different homes as well as the commuting time that many spend on their way to and from work.

2. *Coloring*—Due to immigration and higher birthrates among "minorities," America will have a white minority within perhaps a decade.

3. *Graying*—Because of the large number of "Baby Boomers" (post–World War II babies), we will witness a large segment of population graying. Sometime in the next century, with a large older population, Social Security will require much more than a reasonable labor force can possibly sustain.

4. *Women*—"Today fifty-five percent of women work outside the home, and the Labor Department estimates that the figure will rise to sixty-one

percent."[3] This means that time management, parenting, and volunteerism will experience increased stress.

5. *Pluralism*—Communication choices, like dozens of TV channels, myriads of magazines and newspapers, and the incoming interactive communication age, leave us so bombarded that we often find it difficult to know what and how to believe. Many who call themselves Christian take stands that are contrary to Scripture and to traditional doctrines of the church.

6. *Shifts in segmentation*—Instead of becoming a melting pot, America is increasingly becoming segmented only. Think, for instance, about the family. Instead of only singles and married couples, which you would have had twenty years ago, there are now: singles, nonmarried live-in couples, blended families, single parents, "traditional" marriages, same-sex couples, and others. Each of these segments will tend to feel more comfortable in homogeneous groupings, so churches are increasingly discovering that geography and denomination mean little today. What matters are demographics and psychographics (life orientation).

7. *Short-term commitments*—Churches and institutions are increasingly discovering that people will only do what fulfills them. Patriotism and loyalty are out—self-enhancement and self-fulfillment are in. When times get difficult or an activity stops feeling good, Americans tend to go elsewhere.

8. *Decline in the work ethic*—Work has suffered. Tardiness is rising, as is job turnover. The sense of accomplishment that accompanies hard work is falling.

9. *Conservatism*—As America ages, it becomes more conservative. Yet, being conservative does not mean there is a consistent ideology. Instead, there is a generally cautious approach to life. Positive trends are the increase in family awareness and a slowly decreasing divorce rate.

10. *Cocooning*—Cocooning is the return to the home as the center of life's activities. When we "cocoon," we go home to be refueled and re-energized. This, of course, has had a direct impact on those churches which rely on evening services.

Most readers will readily agree that the ten factors listed above are indeed trends in American culture. We can also observe in them, as Leith

Anderson notes, the end of church as we know it. Gone, maybe forever in America, is denominational loyalty at all costs, as well as single-church loyalty. Most people are stressed out and dealing with rapid change. They want a church experience that is fulfilling and experiential. When a particular church ceases to meet needs, people move on.

In these same factors, however, also exist great possibilities. You can make a strong case for small groups by carefully analyzing each of the ten factors (an exercise you will do at the end of this chapter). For example, the incentive to work (see 8 above) can decline when people feel unstable and unfulfilled. They may feel unstable and unfulfilled because our society is highly mobile and people lack deep, lasting relationships. A small group that *is* community will breed confidence, willingness to take risks, and a sense of security that will carry over into work attitudes.

You can follow the same kind of thought process in examining the other nine societal issues. The result is that you will discover different ways that small groups can become a force in providing stability, security, structure, and societal change.

Biblical Reasons: Many biblical references support small group ministry.[4]

1. The Old Testament framework for the Israelite society revolved completely around the family. Twelve "tribes" traced themselves to patriarchal heads of families. Within the tribes were clans (larger family groupings) followed by households, and then nuclear families. God designed the Israelite nation around the concept of family in order to show the importance of deep, long-lasting relationships.

2. Jesus Christ employed a similar approach. He had an inner circle of 3 close friends, 12 disciples (apostles), a larger circle of perhaps 120 disciples, and the crowds. In his own life, Jesus showed the importance of deep friendships and Christian community. Echoing the Old Testament, Christ called his disciples to " 'love the Lord your God with all your heart and with all your soul and with all your strength and with all your mind'; and, 'Love your neighbor as yourself' " (Luke 10:27).

3. The early church did not have buildings until several centuries after Christ. Since most homes were fairly small and few early believers were affluent, the early church was a small group ministry, and it functioned quite well. These small groups did not need to create megastaff structures in order to meet needs. Everyone received care as part of the body.

4. The New Testament writings, addressed to house churches in different locations, illustrate the need for deep, spiritual relationships.

Theological Reasons: Take any good systematic theology book and attempt to locate a doctrine that has nothing to do with relationships. Every doctrine and every creed speaks to relationships. Unfortunately, by systematizing theology we can forget what we are studying and why we want to know more about God and one another. It is much easier to break relationships down into cold facts on a page than to live in deep relationship with another.

Take the Lord's Supper as an example. It was a meal shared by Jesus Christ with his disciples on the night before he was crucified. He reminded us to "eat this bread and drink this cup" and by it to "proclaim the Lord's death until he comes" (1 Corinthians 11:26). The symbols of bread and wine demonstrate sacrificial love, and the invitation to the table draws believers together in community. How much more relational could Christ have been? Yet we have chosen to fight over issues like transubstantiation and consubstantiation, and over whether clergy are the only ones allowed to serve—so that we don't eat and drink judgment (1 Corinthians 11:29). We cannot lose sight of the fact that the table is a place where people sit in relationship with one another. Such an image belongs not to the high church with cathedral ceilings but to the small group sharing the Christian life together in a humble home.

A more completely developed theological understanding of groups can be found in chapter 7, "What Is Our Purpose?"

What Are the Basic Issues in Small Group Development?

If you ask a representative group of Christians about small group size, meeting patterns, or other issues, you will get a variety of responses. The following list is a sampling of small group issues (in a later chapter, you will get the opportunity to design your own list).

1. What is a small group? It is an intentional gathering of a varied number of people who commit themselves to regular meetings for the purpose of becoming better disciples of Jesus Christ. Notice the elements in this definition. Small groups are intentional. They are relational. They involve regular meetings. The goal is to make disciples for Christ within a varied format and/or framework.

2. *What size is appropriate?* At one time small group leaders would have said three to twelve (including my own *Big Book on Small Groups.*[5] Experience has shown that small groups can be larger than twelve, as long as some smaller grouping (like groups of four) is used for sharing.

3. *How often do groups meet?* Groups can meet as often as they choose. If the intent is to build deep community, however, they should meet at least weekly. Groups that meet biweekly or monthly must take time at each meeting to catch up. A mature group can meet less frequently, especially if the group has multiplied into several groups.

4. *What yearly pattern should groups use?* Groups can continue meeting during Christmas breaks and the summer, but few can sustain themselves during high vacation periods (with one or more individuals absent, the group feels that something is missing). Most groups do not meet during vacation times but wait and start again when everyone can attend.

5. *What is the life cycle of a group?* Most, if not all, groups go through stages. Experts describe a *honeymoon* period at the beginning, followed by a *time of conflict* as the group deals with acceptance and differences. Then, there is an *action* period, followed by *termination* as the group ends. Although some groups may last for many years, most groups have a life cycle of two years or less. The majority of groups will either grow and divide within two years or they will terminate.

6. *Where do groups meet?* Small groups meet anywhere they choose. Some feel most comfortable in the church itself—because the members may live a great distance from one another, or they do not want the pressure of having to clean their houses.

7. *How long are the group meetings?* The ideal meeting length is two hours or less. Groups that meet longer find that members may stop coming because they cannot give so much time and intensity.

8. *What types of groups are there?* Groups take on a variety of forms, including addiction recovery and simple "covenant" groups that meet to grow in faith and knowledge. Some groups involve intense discipleship relationships (sometimes one on one). Others are mission groups that may

minister in a prison. Still others are affinity groups of people with like demographics, gender, life circumstances, or characteristics.

9. How and when do groups take in members? There are three basic types of groups: Open, closed, and open/closed. Open groups are always inviting, making it sometimes difficult to build deep relationships. Closed groups are never open to new members, so they tend to become ingrown. Open/closed groups welcome new members at specific times and close when relationship building is being emphasized. Of the three membership options, the last is the most balanced and probably the most healthy for a group.

10. What do small groups do? Small group activities fall into three areas: (a) loving one another, which includes community building and sharing; (b) loving God, which includes Bible study, prayer, and worship; and (c) loving others, which includes evangelism, mission, and service to the church. The way that groups balance these activities is determined by each group, preferably within the context of a group covenant.

What Issues Are Important in Building Small Group Community?

Although every small group is different, all have one common denominator: the need to build community. What good is a group if everyone hates one another? How much work will a mission team accomplish if it is experiencing discord and disunity?

As important as community building is to small group ministry, many churches do little to equip groups to become a community. When compared with the plethora of books and experts that explore the topic of systematic theology, we find an absence of guidance on the issue of how to build community. As a result, small groups often operate at a deficit in the arena of understanding relationships.

According to Scott Peck in *The Different Drum,* community must be:

Inclusive—accepting of all.
Realistic—containing freedom to express individuality, to be honest, to face facts.
Contemplative—self-examining.

A *safe place*—a place where people can take off their masks.

A *laboratory for personal disarmament*—where we can experiment and take risks.

A *place to fight gracefully*—a place where healthy conflict leads to deeper community.

A *group of all leaders*—each person becoming the maximum person he/she can be.

A *spirit*—a sense of peace and warmth comes over those who participate.[6]

As you look over the list above, you will see how difficult it is to achieve true community in a group. The very thing that people want—intimacy—scares them deeply, and some group members will go to great lengths to protect themselves at the expense of the group.

Knowing more about the issues of community building enhances efforts to build community. To that end, I recommend that you study such issues as spiritual formation in individuals and community building within groups as an aid to your own leadership of groups. For more information on community building, read *The Different Drum*. After reading the book, watch the movie *The Breakfast Club*, the story of five teenagers who spend a day in detention and go through the stages of community development that Peck and others have observed.

What Kinds of Groups Qualify As "Church" Small Groups?

The first answer to this question is "where two or more come together in my name, there I am with them" (Matthew 18:20). Church growth expert Carl George encourages church leaders to move beyond small groups as a program/ministry and to think of small groups as a mind-set.[7] Small group principles should permeate every ministry of the church—from the choir to the staff, from the women's fellowship to the children's ministry. A small group oriented church will have difficulty answering the question, "How many groups do you have?"

At the same time, several types of groups enable churches to fulfill small group goals. The following are several examples:

1. Discipleship groups—emphasizing deep, intense relationships, these groups are usually very small in size (two to four members).

2. *Covenant groups*—the most prominent group type in the church (also called "K-groups," "caring groups," "Bible studies," and a host of other names), these groups typically focus on study, prayer, and community building.

3. *Affinity groups*—these groups possess any of the emphases in this list, and involve people of a common race, gender, age, interest, or other characteristic.

4. *House churches*—often larger than the classic small group, these groups emphasize worship, prayer, and teaching ministry.

5. *Special needs groups*—these groups can involve persons in various types of crises (such as physical, emotional, or relational), such as a recovery group.

6. *Ministry groups*—these teams of individuals serve either within the church or within the community.

7. *Evangelistic groups*—these groups exist in order to evangelize friends and acquaintances.

Should We Train Leaders?

The issue of leadership is central to a church's understanding of small group ministry. In some churches, no one person is chosen as the leader of a group; while in other churches each group has a leader and an apprentice leader who are held highly accountable for the group by the church staff. In between these extremes are other leadership options.

If your church decides not to train leaders, then you must have a viable plan to ensure that each group will begin and mature with either no leadership or with rotating leadership. Churches that use this option will find many pitfalls to overcome, such as how a leaderless group deals with extremely vocal or controlling individuals.

For churches that decide to train leaders, a number of other questions must be answered. First, what kinds of leaders are you looking for? Second, what job description will leaders fulfill? And third, how will you train and support leaders in their different tasks?

In my congregation, leaders are expected to exhibit maturity in Christ and in their relationships. A twelve-week training course based on *The*

Big Book on Small Groups is used to help prepare them for their role as "lay pastor." Leaders are required to fill out monthly reports and to attend meetings with other group leaders for feedback, support, and ongoing training.

How Should Our Church Structure Itself for Small Groups?

The way that a church is structured can help address such issues as how groups are formed, how leaders perceive themselves in relation to the church, and what accountability the church requires of individual small groups. Many churches have chosen, perhaps out of ignorance, to adopt a laissez-faire stance toward small group ministry. Others make small groups the central ministry of the church. Their structure is thoroughly intentional and enforced in a disciplined manner.

Whatever structure your church chooses, oversight and procedure issues should be addressed so that small groups are not an accident, but the result.

Failure to Plan Is Planning to Fail

Imagine two similar churches approaching the idea of small groups at the same time. "First Church" attends a six-hour small group event and adopts the basic model proposed at the seminar. They immediately launch small groups, recruiting twenty individuals to go through an abbreviated leadership training. After six months there are ten groups; after one year there are twelve; after two years there are six; and after three years there are two. When evaluating their church's small group experience, the church leaders conclude that small groups do not work in their situation.

"Second Church" chooses to carefully consider small group issues by using a resource like this one. A team is formed that includes the pastor and a committee of six individuals from the church. They meet together every month for ten months. The team interviews churches with successful small group ministries for input, and churches with failed ministries for advice. They put together a comprehensive plan, which includes specific goals and a leadership handbook. In the second year they choose and train twelve leaders, forming six groups. In the third year they launch five new groups and two of the existing groups multiply. By the fourth year they have twenty groups and their church is experiencing growth.

Why did Second Church thrive while First Church did not? Because they laid a solid foundation under their ministry. Small group ministry's time has come. Yet it is still an unfulfilled potential in many churches because of a lack of knowledge, discipline, and wisdom. Fortunately, the leaders of some of these churches are developing working plans, and instituting change. They are dropping unsuccessful ministry ideas that are past their prime, and adopting the original idea that will never fade—community building through small groups. Sociologically, theologically, and biblically, these churches are on the right track.

Questions to Answer

The questions that follow each chapter are as important as the chapters, perhaps more so. As you answer the questions, you will be putting together a strategy tailor-made for your church, so it is important to answer every question. If you are working through this resource by yourself, you can work at your own pace. If you are part of a team and working through it, do the work on your own and then compare notes at your next meeting.

(Questions that will become a part of your church's strategy manual are in **bold italic**.)

1. Read the ten sociological changes included in this chapter that were taken from Leith Anderson's *Dying for Change*. Choose four of the changes and demonstrate how small groups are a positive response to these changes. Make certain your responses are practical.

a.

b.

c.

d.

2. In summary form, what are ten reasons why small groups are important? (You may combine sociological, theological, ecclesiastical, and biblical reasons.)

a.

b.

c.

d.

e.

f.

g.

h.

i.

j.

3. Spend some time profiling an existing group in your church:

a. size

b. meeting frequency

c. year cycle (what do groups do during the summer? vacations?)

d. life cycle of the group in months/years

e. meeting time/place

f. type of group

g. open, closed, or open/closed, and why

h. what the group has accomplished

i. how people grew from participating in the group

j. connection to the church and its overall ministry

4. Review the above characteristics and then evaluate. Examples: How helpful was the size? Were groups ingrown (closed)? Did some groups try to meet during the summer, and fail? What kinds of basic group decisions could have been better?

5. Reread the definition of a small group in this chapter. How would you define a small group?

6. As you think about the issues related to building true community, name some of the baggage that people in your congregation will bring with them into a group setting (such as insecurity), that will make community building more difficult.

   a.

   b.

   c.

   d.

CHAPTER 2

TWO GROUPS GOING NOWHERE

C hrist Church in Anytown, U.S.A., is an average church. It has a worship service on Sunday morning, followed by Sunday school. It has a small youth group, a women's organization, a choir, and several committees.

It also has two small groups. The first group was started by a young couple who experienced small groups through parachurch ministry while they were in college. The second group started as a pastor's Bible study and continued when he moved to serve another church. Both groups have been around for a number of years, replacing members who move or drop out with others from the church.

An average church performing average ministry in an average town, and two small groups meeting each week. What is wrong with the picture?

Perhaps nothing. But several questions need to be addressed, especially in relation to their small groups. Why are there only two groups? Who decides who can (and *can't*) be in a small group when there are openings? How do they know if the groups are healthy? In what ways do the groups contribute to the life of the church? What happens when a group gets too large? What happens when a difficult person begins to take over a group? Who leads the groups, and how do they lead?

These unaddressed questions are the basis for the title of this chapter. Just as there are stages that a small group will go through when building community, so also are there stages that a church will go through when building a small group ministry. They are:

Stage 0—"two groups going nowhere" (TGGN)

Stage 1—"two groups going somewhere"

Stage 2—"multiplying leaders and groups"

Stage 3—"multiplying churches"

The difference between the first two stages is that in Stage One a church and its leaders have carefully constructed a small group plan (the purpose of this book). In Stage Two a small group mind-set influences the church and more groups begin to spring up. Stage Three is the logical process of churches who benefit from small group ministry. They eventually outgrow their facilities and begin to plant new churches, much like the New Testament church.

Most churches are somewhere between Stage Zero and Stage One, where an unintentional ministry is in place, and the potential exists for harm to be done through small groups.

Identifying Classic Small Group Dysfunction

The possibilities for dysfunction in small groups are numerous. Small groups can split a church, lead individuals into doctrinal error, and promote an ingrown mentality among church members. Some groups have a "teacher" who dominates, and over time he or she can chase others from the group. Other groups contain overly needy individuals who strangle the group with demands it is ill-prepared to handle. Still other groups contain individuals who lack commitment or wander into sin. In other instances small groups can become overly homogeneous and exclude potential members who are different. Group meetings can also provide an opportunity for airing gripes against the church, pastor, and individuals—disguised under the heading of "sharing."

A well-planned strategy cannot always address every problem before it happens. However, if your church has done little or nothing to prepare for a healthy ministry, you can expect to have problems.

Even if your church has a fully functioning small group ministry, it may lack the underlying planning and accountability necessary to guarantee health and growth. The following list of classic dysfunctions can help you identify problems that a better organized ministry can address.

1. Lack of communication. A TGGN (two groups going nowhere) church does not foster healthy interaction between groups and the church and its leadership. One place this weak linkage can appear is between the group leaders and the pastor. If the pastor only hears about small groups "through the grapevine," he or she usually avoids intervening for fear of being accused of meddling. Another weak communication link can appear between the pastor, small groups, and the church at large. If small groups and their underlying themes (like discipleship) are not emphasized from the pulpit, newsletters, bulletins, and fellowship hall conversation, small groups will tend to operate as isolated sectors of the church.

2. Lack of connection. Poor communication fosters a disconnectedness that encourages individualistic behavior. When groups that are not a mainstream part of the church's ministry begin to go their own way, several negative results can follow: (a) Any good done in small groups will feed the church indirectly. Small groups are breeding grounds for service and unconditional love, but most groups seldom initiate congregational service on their own. (b) Any bad qualities of the groups will seep freely into the church. (c) The dangers of schism, laziness, becoming ingrown, doctrinal error, and gossip more easily infiltrate the group.

3. Lack of conviction. Small groups in TGGN churches are free to develop, live, and die on their own. In the absence of direction and discipline, they lack the conviction of ideas and purpose. In other words, they will live much like many Americans tend to live—for today.

What words would you use to describe your small groups and their overall ministry? Would you choose words such as "lack of discipline" and "unfulfilled potential"? If so, your small group ministry lacks the conviction of ideals and purpose.

4. Lack of trained leaders. Trained leaders are not only important; they are indispensable to a healthy, reproducing small group ministry. In TGGN churches, leaders rise from within groups, or are "tabbed" in the same way that other church roles are filled. Yet good small group leaders can act as lay pastors. They provide a level of caring, disciple-making, training, support, and love that would be impossible for a pastor who is ministering to an entire church. Churches that do not nurture their lay pastors are flirting with disaster. They may achieve some measure of success, but one big failure can bring the whole ministry to a crashing halt.

Design Predicts Effectiveness

In the Sermon on the Mount, Jesus taught about a wise man and a foolish man (Matthew 7:24-27). Both men were builders.

The foolish man did not intend for his building to fall down. He intended to construct a durable building. He laid out the walls with care, used the appropriate nails and lumber, and erected the structure. His friends probably helped him move in, and maybe they even held a great celebration for him. Perhaps one of his more blunt, outspoken friends (who has since been removed from any party lists) questioned his choice of building sites. Then came a storm, and the poor man lost his home—his life's work ruined in one great disaster.

The wise man built his house on rock. He possessed the wisdom to not just build a good home, but to put a solid foundation underneath. Consequently, he was ready when the storms came. His house stood firm.

Wise people foresee events. They plan, pray, and discipline themselves in order to reach their goals. Foolish people allow circumstances to dictate their lives. Wise people change the course of history. Foolish people are tossed through history as though they were upon a raft in rapid waters.

Most of us identify more with the foolish man than we do with the wise man. We are more prone to be reactive than proactive. The question we then ask is: Is it possible to reverse poor planning and construct a positive small group ministry in our church? The answer is: Yes, if we closely examine our present plans and alter them in the light of proven principles.

Manageable Ministry

Moses, the great leader of the people of Israel, had a defining moment when his father-in-law, Jethro, stopped by for a visit (Exodus 18). At that point in his career, Moses went each day and sat on a rock in order to serve as a judge among his people. They waited in line from early morning until evening to see Moses.

Jethro said to Moses, "What you are doing is not good. You and these people who come to you will only wear yourselves out. The work is too heavy for you; you cannot handle it alone" (Exodus 18:17-19 paraphrase). Jethro encouraged Moses to break the Israelite nation into thousands, hundreds, fifties, and tens, with godly leaders judging each portion. In this way, nobody would oversee more than a few people, from the smallest leader to the greatest. Communication would flow from bottom to top, and commands could flow from top to bottom.

We call Jethro a good planner. He proposed a system that ensured quality of care, communication, and efficiency. We declare Moses wise for heeding his advice, which he could have ignored.

What implications does Jethro's advice have for small group ministry? First, Jethro gives us a plan for small groups. In his plan each leader worked with only a few people. (In chapter 8, we will learn about the meta-church model, which includes a small group design using Jethro's model). Second, by listening carefully to Jethro's advice and thinking through its implications, Moses saved himself much anguish, and perhaps lengthened his leadership term with the Israelites. The example of his ability to listen encourages us to put aside our pride when addressing questions related to current and future ministry practices. Third, Jethro's advice helps us know how to respond to people who negate planning and designing as nonspiritual tools.

Everything we do has underlying principles and themes—although we may not always be aware of them. Identifying, challenging, and adapting these issues will make us more effective leaders.

The Real Imitation

Walk through a grocery store and look at labels; sometimes designed to mislead, they can also be revealing. A container of chocolate syrup will say "genuine chocolate flavor" (how can an imitation be real?). A can of juice will advertise "100 percent fruit juice"—but only 10 percent of the contents contains the 100 percent fruit juice!

Like the labels above, many churches use the following label for themselves: "Yes, we have small groups." But are the groups accomplishing as much as they can? Is your church only getting a small taste of the benefits of small group ministry? Are your leaders thirsting for the real thing? Your prayer and this planning process hold the key to the kind of exciting, vital ministry that is possible.

The best things in life, like a house built on rock, are accomplished through foresight, planning, prayer, humility, and a relaxed sense of time. If you are going to move from being a TGGN church to one with "Two Groups Going Somewhere," and then to "Multiplying Leaders and Groups," you must begin with an effective plan.

Questions to Answer

1. What is the purpose of this chapter?

2. Reflect on the four small group dysfunctions that distinguish a TGGN church. What are they, and what do they mean?

    a.

    b.

    c.

    d.

3. As you reflect on your church's small group behavior patterns, would you say that they seem like:

    Stage 0—two groups going nowhere? If so, in what ways?

    Stage 1—two groups going somewhere? If so, in what ways?

    Stage 2—multiplying leaders and groups? If so, in what ways?

    State 3—multiplying churches? If so, in what ways?

4. Which of the four small group dysfunctions described in this chapter has your church avoided? not avoided?

5. Telephone at least two churches that have small groups and ask them for information on:

  a. leadership preparation and ongoing requirements

  b. group accountability to, and connection with, the church

  c. their perceived small group ministry strengths and weaknesses

---

Church #1 _____

Person contacted _____

  a. leadership preparation and ongoing requirements:

  b. group accountability to, and connection with, the church:

  c. their perceived strengths and weaknesses:

Church #2 _____

Person contacted _____

  a. leadership preparation and ongoing requirements:

  b. group accountability to, and connection with, the church:

  c. their perceived strengths and weaknesses:

CHAPTER 3

WHAT IS STRATEGIC PLANNING?

W hile working my way through seminary, I participated in an infamous business. For more than a year I sold encyclopedias part time.

I developed my own "pitch" to sell the books. Departing from the company's training, I rewrote the sales talk and did quite well with an approach that combined honesty and personal choice. As you might expect, the company preferred that I follow their script, since they had created sales approaches for every possible situation (we called them "closers," as in closing the deal).

For example, one of our closers was for a "one legger" (a husband whose wife was not present, or vice versa) who balked at spending money without conferring with his or her spouse. We were taught to use this line of conversation:

Well, Mr. Smith, let me ask you a question. What is your absolute dream car?

Mr. Smith: A Jaguar.

Any idea how much a new one would cost?

Mr. Smith: I guess around $50,000.

Okay, Mr. Smith, let us say that you are window shopping at a Jaguar dealership one day. As you enter the building you are startled by lights, band music, and balloons. A beaming man identified as the owner of the establishment approaches you and says: "Congratulations, Mr. Smith. You are the millionth person to enter our doors. You have just won a free Jaguar!" Mr. Smith, would you take the car?

Mr. Smith (falling for my wonderful technique): Without a doubt!

Mr. Smith, there is just one catch. In order to drive the car off the lot you will need to pay sales tax. How much is sales tax in this state?

Mr. Smith (who somehow still does not know what is happening): It is 5 percent.

Right, 5 percent. Let's see now, 5 percent of $50,000 comes to how much? $2,500, right?

Mr. Smith: That is correct. I would get my checkbook right out!

Mr. Smith, you just agreed to spend $2,500 without your wife's approval to buy a luxury item. But you have said you must consult with her before making an investment in these priceless books which will contribute to your welfare, that of your children. . . .

A Plan for Everything

You can see why encyclopedia presentations can be dangerous for potential purchasers! The corporate sales managers had considered every possible sales angle, and because they had developed a thorough sales game plan, they were successful.

While such planning is time consuming, it is also rewarding. The planner who examines her business from as many perspectives as possible is seldom surprised when unexpected situations present themselves.

In a Webster's dictionary, one of the definitions of "strategy" is "careful plan or method, the art of devising or employing plans or stratagems toward a goal." Employing less technical language, a "strategy is a complete managerial game plan."

Notice first that a strategy is complete. The planner considers every possible issue, scenario, and function of the organization in question. Second, planning is managerial. Managers are expected to allocate resources and people to their maximum potential. Managers lead, envision, theorize, communicate, discipline, and guide. Third, planning serves the organization's main purposes (not the planners' own individual ends).

A fourth part of the strategy is the game plan. The game plan explains—in concise terminology—the organization's aims or the primary goal of the business. Major corporations spend a great deal of time and millions of dollars defining their core business strategies. They articulate the plan using *the fewest words possible,* so that *every* employee knows the goals toward which he is aiming. You may notice slogans such as "the best product at the best price in the best manner" when you are shopping. When each employee feels a strong sense of call to the communicated goal, the corporation will experience success.

Like a corporation, the church needs a strong sense of purpose, and church leaders must manage resources and people as if they are business managers or in biblical terminology, "stewards." Churches need common goals and a strong sense of mission. They should function efficiently and effectively. Strategic planning provides the necessary tools to focus energy in a positive direction.

Introduction to Strategic Planning

The planning process involves defining one's purpose and preparing an organization (i.e., large group of individuals) to go in one unified direction. This happens through four basic steps.[1]

1. Define the business and develop a mission statement. This is perhaps the most important step. Imagine a group from a camera manufacturer discussing the purpose of its business. The group might include people from key departments such as accounting, marketing, production, service, and personnel. Asked to develop an all-encompassing corporate mission statement, the different individuals might initially say things appropriate to their own department. Then, as the group continues to work, common trends and themes would be identified.

Here is a typical mission statement: "Our company manufactures and sells photographic products based on inventions of the company in the field of precise photography and light-refracting products, utilizing our inventions in the field of refracted light. The company considers itself engaged in one line of business."

Notice that this manufacturer produces only one product. It is not like some corporations that diversify, for instance, into frozen foods. Instead, this company *emphasizes* its financial and technological energy on developing products for one-step imaging.

Like this manufacturer, the church I served brainstormed activities (ministries) in which it might engage. We created this mission statement: *Our purpose is to be a loving community, finding its greatest joy learning to live God's way.* The key to our church is that *all* of our ministries *become* community. The community we envision is marked by Christian joy and obedience to God's way revealed in Scripture. We can demonstrate how every ministry within the church structure is designed to meet our purpose. You will develop a mission statement for the small group ministry in chapter 7.

2. Craft a strategy that fits the situation and that will produce the targeted performance. Creating a mission statement leads to the question "How will we fulfill it?" This leads you back into your core areas of business to devise ways to succeed.

Imagine a church moving through the strategic planning process. It has developed a mission statement: Our purpose is to create a small group ministry that offers help, recovery, affirmation, and a call to discipleship. The church could then create a strategy that, for example, addresses these possibilities: (1) We will develop a comprehensive recovery ministry; (2) We will create an eight-week leadership training course.

3. Translate the strategy into specific long- and short-term objectives. An objective is a result, a success that leaders want to attain. Objectives flow from the mission statement and strategy. They dictate how one's strategy is to be implemented.

Each objective (or goal) needs to meet certain quantitative and qualitative requirements:

- an objective must be made for *each* key result that is important to success (translated into church language, once you have developed your strategy, you develop objectives for such areas as mission, evangelism, youth, Christian education, and so on).

- each objective should relate to a single, specific topic or area.
- an objective is a result, not an activity (for example, Christian education's objective would *not* be: to provide spiritual nurture for children, youth, and adults. That is already what Christian education does! But what will be the result of the nurture?).
- an objective is measurable (it answers the question, "Did we succeed?").
- an objective has a deadline attached (in our church we have one-, three-, and eight-year goals).
- an objective should be challenging but achievable (winning the world to Christ is a great objective, but not necessarily achievable. But doing evangelism by developing a successful singles ministry may be).

4. Implement the strategy, being open to evaluation, correction, and adjustments. It is hypocritical to think that your plan will be error-free in its first attempt. The small group mission, objectives, and strategy that I now employ in my current church are vastly different from earlier models I attempted. I have made many revisions. Healthy leaders learn to evaluate, correct, and adjust as necessary. This is the subject of chapter 13.

Why Go to All This Trouble?

The four-step process just outlined involves a lot of work. You might be wondering why you need to plan so thoroughly. There are many reasons, but a few will suffice.

First, humans are sinful, and churches involve a complex mix of relationships. We are not always God-centered in the ways that we live and minister to others. We plan because we sin. Imagine leading a church that intentionally develops some comprehensive principles. Two examples might be: *we won't gossip;* and *we will all serve one another.* You could preach these ideas from the pulpit. You could create slogans like "Christians support and serve one another," and hang them as banners around the church. You could teach the principles to young and old alike. You could write small group curricula emphasizing them.

After several years, people will either live out these principles or rebel against them. There is no room for middle ground—for instance, where people gossip and use one another out of ignorance. Your church would be a better place. This is an example of how planning can result in positive change to a church.

Second, Christ followed a very careful script. Throughout the Scriptures we find that Jesus said or did things for purely strategic reasons. For example, recall that he sent out the twelve disciples early in his ministry—to empower them and to teach them reliance on God. Later in his ministry, against all conventional wisdom, he turned his face toward Jerusalem in order to die.

Christ had a mission to bring the kingdom of God to this world. He had objectives to find and train a core of twelve special men; to train a wider circle of disciples in the basics of the faith; to spread the word that the kingdom of God is coming; to die for the sins of the world (to name a few). He had a plan to cross through Samaria, sit at a well, speak to a woman, and bring hope to a whole Samaritan village; to fall asleep during a storm in order to test his disciples' faith.

Jesus also advocated planning. He told the people through the Sermon on the Mount that the wise man built his house (i.e., mission, objectives, lifestyle, strategy) on the principles Christ taught, while the foolish man *heard* the message, but ignored it. In Luke 14 he encouraged people to consider the cost of becoming his disciples. He used the analogy of a person preparing to build a tower by first detailing plans and estimating the costs involved in building. Jesus was not telling churches to develop strategies in these passages. But the principle is transferable: If individuals need to think and plan ahead, organizations need to do so even more.

A Church That Planned

During my travel and speaking engagements, I usually challenge church leaders to spend at least one year developing a small group strategy. At one conference, I promised that I would help launch small groups in any church willing to invest at least one year in planning.

I forgot the promise, but one church did not. Members called me several months later and said, "Well, we did our part; now you do yours!" A traditional congregation from a small denomination, they had gathered a number of people excited about small groups. Meeting faithfully for many months, they had done their homework. Their work was even more remarkable because their church had no pastor during the time that they developed their plan.

I spent a weekend at the church, speaking to the congregation and working with the leaders who had been trained. They were a thoroughly prepared, well educated membership on the brink of major change. It was an exciting time. They had developed a strategy and were prepared to reap its rewards.

Many more churches should join my friends who planned. Those churches currently frustrated with their small group ministry will benefit by developing a comprehensive strategy for promoting and sustaining groups.

Questions to Answer

1. Define strategic planning (your own words).

2. Why is planning important in the church setting?

3. List the four steps of strategic planning, in your own words if possible.

   a.

   b.

   c.

   d.

4. Review the table of contents (or flip through the chapters). Which chapters correlate with which steps?

Step 1 - Chapters _____

Step 2 - Chapters _____

Step 3 - Chapters _____

Step 4 - Chapters _____

5. Optional activity: As a practice exercise, work through the following four steps to see how comfortable you feel. Your answers do not have to be perfect.

a. A possible mission statement for our small group ministry:

b. Some objectives that flow from the mission statement:

c. A strategy for implementing one of the objectives (i.e., leadership development):

d. As you look over the plan you just made, what are potential

STRENGTHS:

WEAKNESSES:

PART TWO
DEVELOPING THE PLAN

CHAPTER 4

WHO ARE WE?

I n the early 1980s, as a youth minister only recently graduated from college, I worked in a church near Philadelphia. I had been working in the church for one year when two events occurred. First, I began sharing an apartment with a youth worker from a successful para-church ministry (a para-church ministry exists outside of a local congregation, usually performing a specific ministry, like Campus Crusade for Christ). And second, I gave the young people in my church a "test" (several short-answer, mostly multiple-choice questions, simply stated and covering the basics of Christianity). I wanted to see what they had learned in the past year.

The test results unnerved me. Few young people, if any, had a clue about how one became a Christian. They did not know the fundamentals of faith, which I (and a host of Sunday school and VBS instructors) had attempted to teach them.

Not sure of my options, I discussed the situation with my new roommate. I wanted to maintain my pride, not ready to admit that my approach was not working (of course, then *I* might be a failure). I complained about "these kids," their lack of spirituality, their apathy, and their rebellion. By complaining, I put the blame on them.

At the same time, I cautiously commended the spiritual depth I observed in my roommate's group. In a very gentle way, he offered a testimony about small groups and disciple-making. He introduced me to a revolutionary new facet of life and ministry. Within one year, our youth group had changed dramatically.

The biggest changes did not involve the youth group. I had to learn a new way of thinking and interacting. I no longer perceived myself as a "grand guru" of kids. I began to see myself as a mentor, disciple-maker, and model. It was a radical change.

Now, imagine trying to change not only the way *you* think about ministry (especially in relation to small groups) but the way the *entire congregation* thinks about it as well. The church already has its established schedule, personality, and perceptions. Imbedded culture is difficult to change.

In order to make a transition to a small group mentality, you will first need to identify both strengths and weaknesses in your church. In this chapter you will examine external factors like schedule, personality, and member involvement. In chapter 5, you will determine the internal values that motivate your church.

Each category we cover (for example, "1. Weekly schedule") corresponds to questions at the end of this chapter.

1. Weekly schedule. The first hurdle to effective small group ministry may be your weekly church schedule. Some congregations that heavily promote programs keep their members overly busy. Members spend too many evenings participating in committees, choirs, church leadership, special events, special events planning, and so forth. Overscheduled people will have no energy for small groups.

2. Church involvement and church needs. Next, examine your church in action—membership, worship attendance, and involvement in the different offerings of the church. Be aware of trends, feelings, and perceptions. One method of doing this is to design a survey and give it to ten people who have left the church, and ten who are inactive. By asking key questions about why they have fallen away, the survey may help you uncover key issues that affect your church's ministry effectiveness.

3. Spiritual growth offerings. The next area of interest is what your church offers in the form of spiritual growth. You will analyze levels of participation, and when and where offerings are held.

Many churches offer Sunday school. You may also consider special evening classes, youth and children's groups that meet at times other than Sunday morning, and special seminars/training events that are offered regularly or periodically. It is helpful, with such an all-encompassing area as "spiritual growth offerings," to include adults, teens, *and* children.

4. *Small group involvement.* Small group analysis can encompass every possible grouping: Special needs groups, recovery groups, Bible study/covenant groups, support groups, prayer groups, and other group types.

5. *Service opportunities.* Then, consider who is involved in committees and service opportunities, such as teaching Sunday school. You should include under this category outreach, follow-up, and evangelism opportunities—such as ministering in a prison, holding services in an area nursing home, and counseling teens. Service opportunities impact the amount of time and energy that people can expend participating in a small group.

6. *Words you would use to describe the church and its ministry.* At this point, you will have uncovered numbers, impressions, facts, and feelings about your church and its ministry. Write some of them down (for example, "traditional" might come to mind; "low percentage of active involvement in Christian growth" might be another). These will help you understand your church better.

7. *Church demographics.* Finally, you will detail the ages, occupations, salaries, family descriptors (such as whether a mother works, or if the family is a blended family), and educational training of those who are active in the life of your church. These will provide additional clues to the viability and strength of your potential small group ministry.

The Wall Came Tumbling Down

These early chapters require patience and diligence. Many churches choose to bypass self-study in favor of starting small groups as quickly as possible. The problem is that building on a shaky foundation (such as an overworked laity) could be dangerous.

On a mission trip to the island of Haiti while I was in college, I had an opportunity to do cinder block laying for three weeks. Not one to lack confidence, I considered myself a master craftsman in no time.

On the last day, my college roommate and I were given the assignment of building a rock retaining wall. We were told to construct three or four layers during the day. The Haitian craftsmen were to finish the wall later.

We began slowly, but early in the day we got bored waiting for one layer to dry—and we began the next layer. Then the next. And the next. We decided to finish the wall by the end of the day.

We reached the very top layer. Then a rumbling in the middle suggested that things were not right. Our survival instincts took over, and we got away from the wall as quickly as possible. The wall came tumbling down—right to the very layer where we got impatient.

Like our rock wall, your work in these early chapters may seem to go slowly. But small groups will not be effective unless you are completely thorough. In most cases, a traditional church will take several years to make the transition to a small group model. It will not happen overnight.

So be patient, mix the mortar, survey the lay of the land, and your time will come!

Questions to Answer

You may need to look at church records, consult the pastor and other church leaders, and interview people who are active, inactive, and who have left the church.

1. Weekly schedule. As completely as possible, make a weekly schedule of all your church's activities. Be sure to include teens' and children's activities, committee meetings, ministry teams, and so on.

WEEKLY SCHEDULE _____ CHURCH
(name)

Worship Service(s):

Sunday:

Monday:

Tuesday:

Wednesday:

Thursday:

Friday:

Saturday:

Monthly special events:

Periodic special events:

2. Church involvement and church needs. Go back to the weekly schedule and write in numbers where appropriate. Notice areas where numbers are strong and where they are weaker (do not draw too many conclusions from numbers, however, since they may not point to spiritual strength). If possible, design a questionnaire (adapt the questions listed below). Give the questionnaire to less active members and those who have left the church. Once you have results, you may choose to write a narrative describing areas in which the church can improve.

Why don't more people participate in the activities offered by our church?_____

What are the strengths of our church? _____

What are our weaknesses?_____

What advice would you give the church leadership about ministry, worship, or anything else? _____

Summary of findings:

3. Spiritual growth offerings. Look at the weekly schedule and identify the spiritual growth offerings (excluding Sunday morning worship). Highlight these, and then tally the numbers:

Adults involved in spiritual growth (average per week) other than worship: ____

Teens involved in spiritual growth other than worship: ____

Children involved in spiritual growth other than worship: ____

Percentage of total participants compared to worship attendance: ____
(for example: 100 participants in an average week compared to 200 in worship = 100/200 = 50%)

4. Small group involvement:

Number of small groups: ____

Total number of small group participants: ____

Percentage of participants compared to worship attendance:
_____

Types of small groups:

5. Service opportunities. Go back to the weekly schedule and plug in numbers of individuals who participate in the various committees listed. Also, make a list of all adults who work in different ministry areas in the church.

6. What descriptive words would you use to describe the church and its ministry (for example, "traditional," "cautious," and so forth)?

7. Church demographics:

  a. Ages of active congregational participants

    ____Under 13

    ____13–19

    ____20–25

    ____25–50

    ____50+

  b. Educational level of active congregational participants, expressed as a percentage

    ____grade school completed

    ____high school completed

    ____college completed

    ____graduate school completed

  c. Occupational breakdown, family units, expressed as a percentage

    ____percentage of white collar

    ____percentage of blue collar

    ____percentage of unemployed

    d. Salary breakdown, family units, expressed as a percentage

        ____percentage of lower and lower middle class
            (salary range $0–$25,000)

        ____percentage middle class
            (salary range $25,000–$60,000)

        ____percentage of upper middle to upper class
            (salary range $60,000+)

    e. Family factors, expressed as a percentage

        ____single parent

        ____intact family (mother and father together)

        ____blended family

        ____two working parents

        ____couples, no children

    f. Overall conclusions. By examining the factors listed above, you can learn a great deal about your congregation's willingness/ability to be involved in small groups. For instance, if both parents in a family are working two jobs, it could be difficult for them to participate.

    What conclusions would you draw about your church, especially as they relate to small groups?

    What grouping(s) do you feel will be most willing to participate in small groups, and why?

CHAPTER 5

WHAT DO WE VALUE?

I once knew a congregation where the pastor frequently employed two themes: "joy" and "family." The themes found their way continually into both his sermons and his private conversations.

However, the pastor himself was, unfortunately, aloof. He kept himself isolated from the congregation. Many members resented him, and rather than experiencing "joy and family," they instead felt bitterness and frustration.

There was a strong minority within the congregation (the traditional 20 percent who did everything) who were fulfilled in their church roles. They were better able to live with the apparent dichotomy between spoken word and reality. Like the pastor, they often spoke of the love and support members gave to one another.

In one sense, they were right. There were evidences of sacrificial love in the church. Unfortunately, a significant portion of the membership missed out on the blessing. Even more saddening, the pastor led himself to believe that joy and family were his church's values, when in fact they were not.

There was a separation between perception and reality. The perception was family, the reality was division. The perception was joy, the reality was bitterness. Because this contradiction was never admitted in public, it continued to exist for years.

The Fragility of Relationships

Relationships are sturdy yet fragile parts of life. They are sturdy because, for example, no matter what happens in my family, my mother is still my mother. They are fragile because sometimes one word, spoken in a certain way, creates conflict or shatters a self-image.

Genesis 2:25 says that "the man and his wife were both naked, and they felt no shame." Adam and Eve were totally transparent, completely known, and still accepted. They had nothing to hide. They could not be rejected, and they were secure.

That status changed when they sinned. Genesis 3:7 says that as soon as they rebelled against God, their eyes were opened and they realized they were naked. Their "ugly" parts became known and they had to hide behind clothing. Today, we hide our insecurities, frailties, and sins behind appearances and masks. In *Biblical Foundations for Small Group Ministry*, Gareth Icenogle calls this the "small group paradox." He identifies sin as the destruction of community, and our lives as a tension between "hunger for intimacy ('it is not good to be alone') and fear of intimacy ('they sewed fig leaves together')."[1]

The church that was previously mentioned had a pastor who hid behind a mirage of his own creating. The church allowed itself to be dragged into the mirage each week, which was for many of its members against their will. While desiring above all else to grow in their faith—and wanting to be obedient to God's Word—they were manipulated by perception. What they claimed to value was not what they valued. What they wanted to be was not what they had become.

It is easy to fool ourselves and others. Many marriages start out in what both partners feel is a positive direction. Over time, however, walls are built and the relationship slowly degenerates. When the partners realize what has happened, the relationship may be irreparably harmed. Intimacy has been lost.

Given our human tendency to be deceived by perception, we must discuss church values. A church "value" is a subconscious perception and motivation that causes a church to act a certain way (for example, a church whose individuals value self-protection will experience gossip, backbiting, territorialism, and other anticommunity behaviors). Some church leaders will find completing this chapter difficult because your church has allowed some negative values to creep into the community.

How Are Values Discovered?

Values-discovery digs beneath the organizational veneer we create. It allows us to isolate the motivations and emphases of our relationships. You uncover values by examining factors that are *external* (building, "dress codes," landscaping); *internal* (feelings, attitudes, perceptions); *structural* (who leads and why, how decisions are made); and *sensitive* (areas of conflict/disagreement, ideas that are "off limits" for one reason or another).

You may wonder how this exercise in values-discovery relates to small group ministry. There are several ways. First, by working through chapters 5 and 6 you will discard negative values and define the values by which you believe your congregation should be operating. Since each small group is a microcosm of the larger church, your small groups will emphasize values pertinent to the entire body.

Second, healthy small groups emphasize positive values. Through small groups you can recreate a church culture from the bottom up.

Third, the values you discover will help you to isolate a "purpose statement" for your ministry (chapter 7). Your entire small group ministry foundation will be built upon your purpose statement.

So How Do We Start?

In his book, *A Church for the 21st Century*, Leith Anderson lays out the following values-finding steps under the heading "What is important to the church?"

A few highly observant insiders may be able to research the church's priorities. If not, an outsider may be needed. There are several places to look.

Where does the church spend money? This is the most measurable piece of the story. Read the budget or review the canceled checks. What percentage of expenditures go to the care of the facility, to programs, to the denomination, to social ministries, to missions, to salaries? . . . What do people fight about? Few fight about matters of low importance. . . . What can't be changed? In some churches it is the platform furniture. . . . What are the symbols? The cross?[2]

It takes work to find a church's values. Leaf through church minutes (this is a wonderful place to begin, because minutes isolate things that occupy the church's leadership attention); dig up annual reports and budgets; walk through the church observing its physical attributes; and bring in outside observers to give honest and objective assessments according to certain criteria.

Here are some of the steps which you will follow in your work.

1. Examine the work you have done in chapter 4 for keys and trends. For instance, if you used a word like "traditional" to describe your church, then you may be a church that values tradition.

2. Describe your church "type." The following are designations from *A Church for the 21st Century*. Your church may be a combination of two or more:

   a. "family farm"—Typically small, families together for generations, not particularly enthusiastic about allowing "outsiders" to become church leaders.
   b. "school"—Churches that emphasize teaching and doctrine.
   c. "franchise"—Churches within strong denominations that encourage/require a homogeneous belief system, structure, and leadership.
   d. "general store"—A church that fills a unique niche. Typically small to medium size, it has some ministries but not many that are specialized (youth group, singles group, etc.).
   e. "shopping mall"—Large, attractive, convenient, these churches provide a wide variety of services to a broad cross-section of individuals.
   f. "specialty shop"—These churches reach out to a particular kind of person, such as vacationers or persons of a particular nationality (for example, Korean).
   g. "haunted house"—Big imposing churches, now mostly empty.

3. Discern what is important to your church, noting key ideas in church minutes, budgets, annual reports, and conversations. What topics occupy church's leaders' attention, cause the most arguments, and might never be changed?

4. Locate an outside, objective observer. Invite him/her/them to church in order to help you answer these questions:

   a. How would you describe the building? Grounds?
   b. How did you feel entering the church? Roaming the halls? Meeting people? Entering worship? During worship? Following worship?

c. How would you describe the church, its people, its emphases?

d. What type of person do you think will be attracted to this church, and why?

5. Look at each ministry for key ideas that they convey. For example, perhaps when you look at adult education the word "lecture" comes to mind. Maybe "curriculum" is the most important part of the children's ministries. Or "fun" for the youth ministry. Or "liturgical" for worship. Make sure that you can describe at least one value for each ministry.

6. Finally, examine the small group ministry. What do the small groups value? What happens in small groups, and why?

The Starting Point of Change: Confession

Great change must occur in order to move a church from a program orientation to a small group mind-set. For many churches the concepts of mutual accountability and shared learning are foreign. Before churches change, they must first understand what thoughts occupy their minds. Self study and confession offer a starting point for organizational change and growth.

The prophet Jeremiah said the following about self-deceit:

> The heart is deceitful above all things
> and beyond cure,
> Who can understand it?

> "I the LORD search the heart
> and examine the mind,
> to reward a man according to his conduct,
> according to what his deeds deserve."
> (Jeremiah 17:9-10)

The church spoken about in the beginning of the chapter rarely saw people come to make professions of faith. The values of the church did not match its reality of the church. People sensed hypocrisy.

The church I currently serve, *without* a great evangelistic emphasis but with a disciplined approach to values, celebrates people coming to an increase in faith regularly. Is it because we are better? Not at all—we just know what we value.

Questions to Answer

1. What is a "value"?

2. Discover your church's values:

a. Look over your answers to the questions in chapter 4, and attempt to assign appropriate values for its:

—schedule (busy, relaxed?):
—overall "feel":
—predominant age of the congregation, and what might
   that age value?

b. Describe your church "type" (for descriptions, see chapter 5): Is your church a family farm; school; franchise; general store; shopping mall; specialty shop; haunted house? or a combination?

c. Discern what is important to your church by examining the following:

—church minutes (what occupies the most time, attention, and
   paper)?

—budget (what is the majority of money spent on? how much is
   spent maintaining, how much on growth?):

—annual reports (what ideas seem to flow from report to report;
   what ministries are given the highest priority?):

—conversations with church members (what is important to them?
   what do they think is important to the church?):

d. Invite an outside observer into your church. Ask his/her response to these questions:

—how would you describe the buildings? grounds?
   (what values are inherent in the description?)
—how did you feel entering the church?

roaming the halls?

meeting people?

entering worship?

during worship?

after worship?

—how would you describe the church, its people, its focus/emphases (i.e., what do you perceive to be our values?)?

—what type of person would be attracted to this church?

e. Look at each ministry specifically for keys and trends. Describe one value that seems to be important to each ministry:
   —Adult education:
   —Worship:
   —Children's ministry:
   —Youth ministry:
   —Committee involvement:
   —Staff relationships:
   —Finances:
   —Maintenance/buildings:
   —Other (personnel, long-range planning, etc.):

f. Examine small groups specifically.
   —What do the current small groups value, and why?

3. Summarize your findings (combine and condense where possible). What does your church value?

CHAPTER 6

WHAT DO WE WANT TO VALUE?

Changing the direction of a church requires commitment, perseverance, and a solid plan. In *A Church for the 21st Century,* Leith Anderson provides a starting point for churches willing to change:

> Each church needs to define health for itself. That comes through a process of comparison, consultation, and self-evaluation. Comparison is made with other churches, especially healthy ones. Consultation with outsiders helps us see ourselves as others see us. Self-evaluation is applying insider's insights to the comparisons and consultations.
>
> An individual might conclude that health for me at my age and with my setting is that I should weigh 175 pounds, have a normal body temperature of 98.6, a pulse of 72, 20/20 vision with contact lenses, and run a mile in 7 minutes. For a church it might be that health for us is an annual growth rate of 5 percent, with half of that growth coming through evangelism, annual offerings of $1,000 per person (based on average Sunday morning worship attendance), 40 percent of adults in small-group Bible studies, and average pastoral tenure of at least nine years.[1]

In the last chapter you identified the values that motivate behavior in your church. Some of which are positive and should remain in place, while others need to be changed. In this chapter you will design the "ideal" small group ministry (step 1). Then, you will create a set of specific, compre-

65

hensive ministry values (steps 2 and 3). Finally (step 4), you will craft a *vision statement* encompassing the entire ministry. In later chapters you will decide on the method you will use to transition your church from its current situation to where you believe it should be.

Step 1. Envision the Ideal Small Group Ministry

Imagine a new person who walks into a healthy church for the first time. How will that congregation minister to that person through its small groups? How will they assimilate her? How will they guide her in her journey of faith?

There are several church "stops" that a person may visit on her way to Christian maturity. They are:

- First-time visitor
- Christian/assimilated member
- Recovery from addiction, abuse, grief, divorce, and so forth
- Support during various life stages (i.e., parenting)
- Discipleship
- Leadership development
- Evangelism and outreach
- Mission involvement

At the end of this chapter, these categories (along with other relevant categories you may choose to add, such as "youth ministry" and "children's ministry") appear in outline form. You will create vision statements for each one.

Successful dreaming does not require you to be specific or realistic. Allow yourself the privilege of dreaming about how things can be. If you cannot develop a vision for a particular category, ask people in your church, another church, or even the community for help. The following two samples illustrate the process of creating vision:

First-time visitor—Most people who enter a church are insecure, even if they have friends who attend the church. The role of the church is to welcome newcomers and provide a safe growth environment. Our vision for small group assimilation will be:

Our small group ministry is committed to reaching out to newcomers by emphasizing caring community building within groups—demonstrating the value we place on individuals; encouraging groups to invite newcomers, and newcomers to join groups; and making small group ministry highly, and physically, visible in the church (i.e., bulletin boards) so that people know we want them to be involved.

Recovery from addictions or grief—The perception exists in some places that the church does not help people who are hurting. There are many ways that a congregation can ignore and deny pain: A well-dressed, "and how are you today" surface culture; withdrawing from somebody who has lost a loved one; and expressed horror when it is discovered that someone is addicted or has been abused.

Many churches discover that through a recovery ministry individuals are able to put their faith in Jesus Christ and become involved in the church. Christian Twelve Step groups are forming all over the country, using such names as "overcomers" and "more than conquerors," and they are meeting a wide range of needs.

Most of the work in recovery and addition ministry is being done in small groups. A vision for your church might be:

Our small group ministry will provide opportunities for individuals with a variety of addictions, abuses, and traumas to find complete healing through a supportive and loving community, led by trained leaders.

Step 2. List the Values Undergirding the Ideal Design

The next step is to identify the values that undergird your vision. To discover the values, read through your vision statements and note important ideas, concepts, and motivations. Here are several examples of values you may find underlying a small group ministry:

- We value newcomers and want to relate to them in community.
- We expect a high level of commitment from our members.
- We challenge our members to make a commitment to Jesus Christ.
- We value those who are in pain and who are struggling in faith and life.
- We urge our members and friends to submit to the Lordship of Jesus Christ.
- We value people and will invest time, energy, and leadership helping them to grow.

Step 3. Refine and Create a Set of Values

Next, look over the values you have listed and do two things. First, add any values that are missing. Second, condense the ideas so that the list is clear.

What follows is a list of values developed in 1994 for the church I currently serve. Although these values are for the entire church, they offer a point of comparison for the set of values you will develop:

We value

a. in everything a worshiping, loving, and serving community.
b. a superior level of member care with support, counsel and help in crisis.
c. a church where young people and children are loved, nurtured, and challenged.
d. a genuine, celebrative worship service with full participation by all in adoration of God.
e. an empowering, equipping, and energizing style of preaching and teaching.
f. streamlined decision making that emphasizes ministry, not committees.
g. creative, articulate, personal outreach and mission.
h. all members using their spiritual gifts in service to the body of Christ.
i. small groups that allow for a decentralized, mobilized army of ministry leaders.
j. prayer that gives focus to all that we do.
k. the family, which will be strengthened through involvement in our church.

Step 4. Develop a Vision Statement

Writing a vision statement requires identifying "core" concepts which are important to the ministry. This is an intermediate step to developing a one-sentence purpose statement, which you will do in chapter 7.

Through your work, you may develop a vision statement similar to the following:

We are committed to a strong, dynamic small group ministry that has a significant impact on:

a. newcomers entering our church.
b. those who need healing and support.
c. the overall church as we grow from the "bottom up."

d. the areas of disciple-making, worship, prayer, mission, and evangelism.
e. our community as the church moves beyond the church walls.
f. church and world as we train and mobilize leaders to make a difference.

Seeing the Difference

A traditional mainline church with a bloated leadership structure and powerless laity decided it wanted to make a change. Its leadership team spent one year working through the process laid out in this resource. When the strategy was complete, the pastor approached the various boards and committees within the church for their support. Potential small group leaders were invited to an all day orientation held on a Saturday. Thirty-six leaders attended.

Following the orientation, twenty leaders attended extended training. In the first year, ten groups were formed. In the second year, another ten groups were formed. Over time, the church became a warm, inviting community. People learned to pray, read scripture, lead, and participate. The church's culture changed and the lives of its members were affected—all because the church invested in a new vision.

Many churches settle for doing ordinary things according to yesterday's values. Others decide that they want to make significant changes. Strong values, a powerful vision and discipline will help you to make the change. You will doubtless find it difficult to adopt new values, but small groups can help to turn the whole course of your church slowly, and steadily, in a new direction. The end result is a well-designed ministry that will do great things for Christ and his kingdom.

Questions to Answer

1. Design the ideal small group ministry. For each of the following, list several vision ideas (how can small groups influence this area "in the ideal"?):

a. First-time visitor:

b. Christian/assimilated member:

c. Recovery:

d. Support:

e. Discipleship:

f. Leadership development:

g. Evangelism and outreach:

h. Mission involvement:

i. Other:

2. List the values undergirding your ideal design. (Review the ideas listed under question 1.) (List all values even when they occur more than once.)
   Example: We value newcomers and want to relate in community with them.

3. Refine the list under question 2. Create a set of values under-girding the emerging small group ministry in your church (add values that appear missing as well). Our small group ministries value:

4. Develop a vision statement for the small group ministry. Isolate the significant areas of ministry that small groups will be involved in (i.e., recovery, discipleship, etc.) and devise a statement for each.

CHAPTER 7

WHAT IS OUR PURPOSE?

S tudy groups. Recovery groups. Wholeness groups. Support groups. Mission groups. Evangelistic groups. House churches. Ministry groups. Affinity groups.

In the church that I serve, we allow for each of these group types. At the same time, we view each group as part of our overall small group ministry. Every leader goes through training. Every group fulfills the same purpose.

We now know *why* we do small group ministry, so that every part makes sense within the whole. Without a cohesive vision of ministry, we might have ten groups doing different things, going in ten different directions.

We have answered the simple question "why small groups"? We have given our leaders a sense of purpose for the overall ministry. In this chapter we will develop a statement of purpose. This one brief statement will summarize all the previous work, and will dictate the rest of our planning.

In order to help you observe the process of purpose-forming, the remainder of the chapter will illustrate the development of my own statement of purpose.

Whatever Happened to Relationships?

One Sunday my fiancée, Karen (now my wife), and I sat together in a pew, having entered church prepared for worship. Enjoying the warmth of the moment, I put my arm around her. We shared our thoughts with faces pressed closely together.

A boisterous friend interrupted our quiet moment when he stopped to congratulate us on our engagement. As he prepared to move away, he said in a voice loud enough to be heard by others: "Just wait until you have been married for a year or two—you will not even be sitting on the same pew!"

Others laughed, but I did not. In my ministry I work every day with relationships full of broken promises, unfulfilled longings, and hurts that a heart cannot express.

I listen to words like his with fear. I recall directing my fear toward my upcoming marriage. Would my marriage turn out like his—where he and his wife only "communicated" when making each other look foolish? Would Karen and I end up sitting on opposite sides of the church? Would my marriage disintegrate so that we would one day say "we have grown apart and have fallen out of love"? Would any children we bore have to suffer from our broken relationship?

Humans build relationships because we believe they offer healing and wholeness. Why then do so many people experience alienation instead? There are many things that happen when we build relationships. We find things we don't like about one another; we disagree; we withhold important feelings or thoughts from one another; we find out that honesty hurts; we stop communicating. It's not hard to see why many people are not fulfilled in their closest relationships.

"They Were Naked"

Relationships were not always as we know them. In an environment that we cannot imagine, as recorded in Genesis 2, God created man and woman and placed them in a beautiful garden. They worked together and ruled over God's earth. They shared their love for God in complete, uncluttered, shame-free unity. Their God-given joy far surpasses anything we have experienced in our deepest moment of worship.

And they were naked—completely naked—without attention being drawn to the fact. They were open books to one another, not just physically but emotionally, mentally, and spiritually as well. In the absence of sin, judgment did not exist. No critical eyes to see the weight gain, the tear-stained face, the insecurity.

Imagine how free they were to explore and enjoy their world! No shopping for clothes to help "make a statement." No makeup was needed to cover their flaws. No wondering what others were thinking. No time was wasted in gossip, or worrying about manners and customs.

"They Realized They Were Naked"

As Genesis 3 notes, the idyllic world did not exist for long. Satan entered the picture. Preying upon the innocence of the man and woman, he teased them into fatally damaging their greatest asset—their relationships.

As they blindly followed a new master, their world began to unravel. Adam looked at Eve with new critical eyes. Eve looked at Adam in the same way. Then, "the eyes of both of them were opened, and they realized they were naked."

Destroyed in that one fatal moment in history was absolute security, intimacy, and unity. We have lost the pure joy of being ourselves and finding ourselves totally and unconditionally accepted.

Genesis 3 discloses the nature of evil: Evil separates us from God and from one another. First, Satan pursued our relationship with God. He introduced the first doubt (are you *sure* that God is so trustworthy—after all, you are naked and so gullible?). That doubt gave birth to sin (if we eat this fruit we shall be as wise as God!).

Satan knew that once our relationship with God was damaged, our human relationships would naturally follow. We observe our forefather and foremother with horror as they feebly attempt to cover themselves. Working together, they sewed fig leaves into garments that masked their nakedness. Then, they hid from God.

Upon finding them hiding pitifully among the bushes, God confronted them. Satan gleefully watched as the man and woman turned on one another. The great conflict of the ages was set in motion. The result of sin is the undermining of relationships and the permanent loss of perfect intimacy on earth.

The Evidence of Evil

So we live a dichotomy: Created for the purposes of intimacy and interdependence, yet we constantly struggle against isolation and alienation.

Think about the struggles of children. They must create an identity and locate their niche in the world. But the world can be a cruel place. Only the strong survive. Think of the pain caused by being chosen last for a team. Imagine how they feel when others make fun of a birthmark. Many children are abused verbally, physically, and sexually. A great many more experience the trauma of divorce.

Childhood is but a precursor for the struggles of adolescence: Wanting to fit in and be popular; worrying about weight and pimples; growing up, dealing with bodily changes; making friends, then seeing those relationships disperse like clouds; facing a future that is uncertain at best; dealing with family issues that complicate life; dating; and facing issues such as sex and sexuality.

Many adults feel that the pain of childhood pales in comparison to adulthood: Facing responsibility and making major decisions; attempting to raise children in a broken world; fighting the problems caused by a 50 percent divorce rate; struggling with bills and the expectations created by a materialistic society; working in imperfect work environments.

These are only a few of the relational problems that we face every day. There are many, many more. Each sin, insecurity, rebellion, and addiction points to one problem—the loss of intimacy which is described in Genesis.

The Root Problem

Evil destroys community, but God builds bridges that lead to community. God allowed Adam and Eve to live together and to interact with God even after sin, and sent Jesus Christ so that the earth would have a human, relational touch. Through Scripture God and the plan for humanity is revealed.

Not enough humans have heard God's call to love with their hearts and souls and minds and strength. We have not loved our neighbors as ourselves (as Jesus says, "All the Law and the Prophets hang on these two commandments" [Matthew 22:40]). Even in the church, where the community of faith has been called to a new relationship, the evidence of evil's power is painfully obvious. We claim to adopt God's plan for the world while allowing our relationships to crumble. Churches are well known for controversy, division, in-fighting, and gossip. We do not seem to hear God's call to intimacy, which begins in Genesis 2, continues through Jesus

Christ, and will climax in fulfillment of the prophecies of justice and mercy in Revelation.

Turning the Corner

In *The Great Divorce*, C. S. Lewis pictured himself on a fictional bus ride with a group of people leaving hell to explore heaven. Lewis' classic book tracks various individuals on that bus as they explore the fringe of heaven. During the trip, Lewis speaks with a man about the place they have left.

"It seems the deuce of a town," I volunteered, "and that's what I can't understand. The parts of it that I saw were so empty. Was there once a much larger population?"

"Not at all," said my neighbor. "The trouble is that they're so quarrel-some. As soon as anyone arrives he settles in some street. Before he's been there twenty-four hours he quarrels with his neighbor. Before the week is over he's quarreled so badly that he decides to move. Very likely he finds the next street empty because all of the people there have quarrelled with *their* neighbors—and moved. So he settles in. If by any chance the street is full, he goes further. But even if he stays, it makes no odds. He's sure to have another quarrel pretty soon and then he'll move on again. Finally he'll move right out to the edge of the town and build a new house. You see, it's easy here. You've only got to *think* a house and there it is. That's how the town keeps on growing."

"Leaving more and more empty streets?"

"That's right. And time's sort of odd here. That place where we caught the bus is thousands of miles from the Civic Centre where all the newcomers arrive from earth. All the people you've met were living near the bus stop: but they'd taken centuries—of our time—to get there, by gradual removals."

"And what about the earlier arrivals? I mean—there must be people who came from earth to your town even longer ago."

"That's right. There are. They've been moving on and on. Getting further apart. They're so far off by now that they could never think of coming to the bus stop at all. Astronomical distances. . . ."[1]

The earth is full of people building fantasy worlds that attempt to negate the brokenness of relationships. New religions and philosophies con-stantly spring up—yet we are no closer to solving the problems of humanity than we were hundreds of years ago. While we can now study society with sophisticated social science methodology, we have come closer to destroying ourselves (i.e., the atom and hydrogen bombs, germ and biological warfare, etc.) than at any point in our history.

C. S. Lewis has located the core of the human problem: *isolation.*

My Purpose Statement

This discussion leads to my statement of purpose for small group ministry of which the restoration of relationships is the focus. Satan sought to destroy them in the garden, but we must attempt to rebuild them with the help of God.

Here are a few possible purpose statements:

- "Our purpose in small group ministry is to build a loving community patterned according to the love defined and demonstrated through Christ in Scripture."
- "Our purpose is to learn to love God and one another in true Christian community."
- "Our purpose is to make disciples who love God with heart, soul, mind, and strength, and who love neighbor as self."
- "Our purpose is to 'Reverse the Curse,' aiming to restore intimacy with God and others."

Is It All-Encompassing?

There are several questions that may come to mind when you read the possible purpose statements that appear above:

1. Where is Jesus Christ in the purpose statement (after all, he is the focal point of salvation history)? He is present in a number of ways. First, intimacy with God only becomes possible when a person has asked Jesus Christ to be his or her Savior. Salvation is the first step toward restored intimacy. Second, Jesus modeled intimate relationships on earth. He lived in constant communion with the Father, often creating time to be with God in prayer and solitude. He valued his relationships with the disciples above all earthly relationships. He even had an inner circle of three best friends—Peter, James, and John. Third, Jesus summed up the whole

message of the Old Testament Scriptures when he said, " 'Love the Lord your God with all your heart and with all your soul and with all your mind.' This is the first and greatest commandment. And the second is like it: 'Love your neighbor as yourself.' All the Law and the Prophets hang on these two commandments" (Matthew 22:37-40).

2. Is importance given to building a faith foundation rooted in doctrine and theology? Moreover: What is the purpose of doctrine and theology? They are meant to teach us truths about God, our world, ourselves and our sinful nature. Doctrine and theology are a systematic attempt to describe healthy relationships. They are tools that must lead us into a richer relationship with God, ourselves, and others.

3. What of study, prayer, evangelism, and the other elements of small groups? The purpose of study is to educate us about living in relationship. Prayer and worship *are* relationship. Evangelism is a way of sharing the blessing of our faith relationships (i.e., the Good News) with others.

There are more questions that we can ask, but these demonstrate how to "test" your statement of purpose.

Questions to Answer

1. Put your Mission Statement from chapter 6 in this space.

2. *By combining and simplifying your ideas, prepare a one-sentence statement of purpose for your small group ministry.*

3. *Now, reread the values listed in chapter 6. Does your purpose statement encompass all of them? Continue editing your statement until it does.*

CHAPTER 8

WHAT IS OUR STRATEGY?

In 1862 the Union general George McClellan led a massive army to the outskirts of the Richmond, Virginia, headquarters of the Confederacy. He hoped to put an early end to the war. In response, Confederate general Robert E. Lee performed a strange, but brilliant, maneuver. He sent his finest general, Stonewall Jackson, marching north into the Shenandoah Valley of Virginia. McClellan (a cautious general who sometimes overestimated the forces facing him) assumed that Jackson was marching on Washington with a large army. He dispatched three armies, each under capable leaders, to head Jackson off and save Washington.

In a brilliant campaign, Jackson convinced each of the generals that his forces were superior. In fact he had a poorly outfitted but disciplined band of men who were outnumbered by *each* of the armies they faced. Jackson's men hit each army separately and hard, forcing them to retreat. McClellan had to send another large piece of his army back to defend Washington. His campaign to capture Richmond failed.

The Shenandoah Campaign demonstrates what happens when a numerically inferior force with great confidence meets a numerically superior force with a defensive mind-set. If we look at the campaign as a model it teaches us values such as the power of discipline, self-confidence, and sacrificial discipleship (Jackson's men revered him); and the brilliance of effective strategy.

The church after twenty centuries acts much like the Union army of 1862. We are much larger than we realize. We possess more resources than we can imagine. Yet we consistently overestimate our "enemies." We have adopted a defensive posture. We are in no condition to tackle the twenty-first century. We have not developed a ministry plan to consistently reach teens and young adults. Members of the "Generation X" often believe the church is irrelevant. Seventy-five percent of churches have reached a plateau or are in decline. Mainline churches are in-fighting themselves into obsolescence. The church appears to be in a long, slow process of retreat.

In order to survive and move into the twenty-first century, the church must adopt a revolutionary mind-set. We must begin to embrace strong will, discipline, action, intensive discipleship, and a can-do attitude. To accomplish the turn-around, the church must break itself into smaller units. It must train effective leaders and prepare itself for "battle."

To accomplish its objectives, the church must have a plan.

Reviewing the Process

In the previous four chapters you began to develop your strategy. As you may recall from chapter 3, there are four stages in the planning process:

Stage 1—define the business and make a mission statement.

Stage 2—craft a strategy that fits the situation and will produce the targeted performance.

Stage 3—translate the mission into specific long- and short-term objectives.

Stage 4—implement the strategy, being open to evaluation, correction, and adjustments.

You have worked exclusively in the realm of defining your purpose and creating a vision statement. We now move to strategy crafting.

Laying Out Strategy

Finalizing your strategy will involve four steps:

1. Design the Ideal Ministry—using the same thought process employed in chapter 6 to create your vision for ministry.

2. Structure the Ideal Ministry—showing how small groups are connected to the church.

3. Complete Basic Small Group Information—completing questions raised in chapter 2.

4. Answer the Leadership Question (see chapter 9).

Strategy Formulation Step 1
Design the Ideal Ministry

In chapter 6 you crafted a vision for the different areas of ministry that small groups can influence. You may have chosen some or all of those listed: first-time visitor; assimilated member; recovery; support; discipleship; leadership development; evangelism and mission; mission involvement; or created your own. This step will involve each of the categories you chose. However, this time you will add the specifics of ministry. Be as clear, concise, and realistic as possible. As you work, make sure that your results are ready to transfer to the final document you create in chapter 11. Here are samples to demonstrate the process:

1. First-time visitor. Most persons are insecure when they enter a church for the first time. Small groups can help visitors find a church home:

a. Every small group will use the "empty chair" (a well-known small group ministry, "Serendipity," is credited with starting this idea). Every small group meeting will include an empty chair. The group then prays for the Lord to spiritually prepare the person who is to sit in that chair.

b. Every small group will be "open" during significant times in the year, ready to invite newcomers into the group.

c. The pastor(s)/head of the follow-up committee will work closely with small group leaders to provide names of potential invitees.

d. In the entry or narthex of the church, there will be a noticeable and sharp visual display about small group ministry with brochures and response forms available. In addition, small groups will maintain high profile through sermons, bulletins, and newsletters.

2. Christian-assimilated member. In his book titled *New Member Assimilation,* Joel Heck identifies characteristics of an assimilated member, including: Regular attendance at worship; participation in the life of the church; and regular giving. His most significant characteristic: An assimilated person has six close friends in the church. According to his criterion, many people in existing membership roles are not assimilated. Small groups can facilitate the process of assimilation by:

a. Having every New Member Course involve eight weeks of small group participation under the direction of trained leaders. At the end of the course, a group may elect to stay together, or the individual members may choose to join other groups.

b. Including in every New Member Course a discussion on how to give one's life to Christ. Opportunity will be given—in nonthreatening ways—to share our life stories.

c. Including a spiritual gift questionnaire in the New Member Course. When a person joins the church, she will commit to serving Christ and the church in at least one gift-based capacity.

d. Considering every New Member Course as a recruiting ground for small groups. At least one session in the course will address small group ministry.

3. *Working through recovery issues.* Many people are dealing with recovery issues. Some may be confronting memories of physical and/or sexual abuse experienced as a child. Others are facing grief, divorce, alcohol/drug abuse, or other issues.

Some churches choose to ignore people who are in pain, leaving them to counselors and therapy groups. These churches are missing a golden opportunity to do that which Christ calls the church to do. (Remember, Jesus said on several occasions, he came for the "sick," not the healthy). Churches that ignore the needs of persons involved in recovery are not grasping a major part of recovery ministry—that the issues are all-consuming. Until people experience healing, their service to the church and world will be minimized.

a. Our church will develop a community needs survey so that we can target recovery needs that are currently unaddressed within the faith community.

b. We will offer recovery groups including Twelve Step and trauma recovery groups. The groups will be led by experienced, trained leaders who can facilitate the recovery process.

c. We will encourage individuals who participate in recovery groups eventually to mainstream into other small groups and/or to become trained recovery group leaders.

d. The recovery groups will work in partnership with organizations in the community where possible, using materials prepared by experts. Our groups will without reservation affirm that Jesus Christ is our "higher power."

4. Receiving support. Support groups perform a meaningful ministry service. They put individuals together into homogeneous groups such as those involving mothers, couples, widows/widowers, pastors, people helpers, accountants, and others.

a. Our church will develop a community needs survey so that we can target support needs that are currently unaddressed within the faith community.

b. Support groups are encouraged to use materials from our small groups resource library.

c. Support groups are encouraged to study broad discipleship issues (not narrow, homogeneous needs), so that they do not become stuck on their circumstances and stagnant in their relationships.

5. Becoming a disciple. The goal of every small group is to make disciples who become more like Jesus Christ.

a. Disciples are made in community. We will focus all of our groups on building healthy relationships with God, self, the community of faith, and the world.

b. The church will develop a library of positive, doctrinally sound books, Bible study resources, Bible helps, and other resources to be used by small groups.

c. Every small group leader will participate in monthly meetings for accountability, support, fellowship, and problem solving—enabling him or her to be a more effective disciple-maker.

d. We encourage two disciplines to avoid becoming ingrown. First, all groups will be expected to invite newcomers. Second, groups will develop a service to the church and/or community, at least four times per year, according to the model developed by Steve Sjogren in *Conspiracy of Kindness* (Vine Books).

e. We will encourage groups larger than twelve to birth a new group. The birthing process will involve pastoral leadership as necessary.

6. Becoming a leader (a complete strategy is developed in chapter 9). A Christian leader is a catalyst who enables others to grow relationally, spiritually, and mentally.

a. Every person in a group will have a useful group role. Group leaders will be trained to allow members to help with fellowship, worship, prayer, timekeeping, and sharing.

b. Every small group leader will be responsible for finding an "apprentice" leader and preparing that person for eventual group leadership.

c. We will train all small group leaders using *The Big Book on Small Groups* (InterVarsity Press) and our church strategy.

d. Every small group leader will complete regularly scheduled reports and attend monthly small group leader meetings.

7. *Making a difference through evangelism/outreach.* People who grow and submit to Christ begin to care for those who may not know Christ, and are in need.

a. Every group will include an "empty chair" at each meeting, and will pray for the person who is to fill it.

b. Every group will be encouraged to begin praying for specific friends, relatives, and neighbors who do not know Christ.

c. Certain leaders with a gift for evangelism will be encouraged to begin evangelistic Bible studies using the *Your Home, a Lighthouse* model (NavPress).

d. Small groups will participate in low-risk, high-grace service projects according to the model developed in *Conspiracy of Kindness*.

8. *Identifying with God's plan for the world: mission.* Evangelism occurs within our natural web of relationships. Mission occurs when a person intentionally crosses cultures locally, nationally, or internationally. Some groups may want to become involved in local mission and will become service groups. Others may support and pray for missionaries. Some will choose to go on short-term mission trips.

a. Every small group will be apprised of mission opportunities available locally, nationally, and internationally.

b. Every small group will be encouraged to participate in mission at some level, no matter how small.

c. A group that wants to be regarded as a service group and to be funded through church mission must complete an application and submit it for consideration by the church leadership.

Strategy Formulation Step 2
Structure the Ideal Ministry

There are several ways that you may structure small group ministry. Choose the one that best fits your situation, or create your own adaptation. Here are some of the possibilities.

1. Meta-church design—The meta-church model was created by church growth expert Carl George. You can find out more about this model by reading *Prepare Your Church for the Future* (Regal Books). The meta model is a model for the entire church.

In the meta-model, there are three levels of ministry: celebration, congregation, and cell. Celebration refers to the church gathered in worship. Congregation represents larger groupings within the church, like a women's fellowship or a singles ministry. However, the congregation's primary purpose is to feed individuals into small groups (cell), the building block of the meta-church. For a meta-church to succeed, small group thinking must permeate all of its ministries.

The small group design for meta (which, incidentally, uses Roman numerals to indicate the size of the groups), looks like this:

D—Staff pastor (meta system calls this a "District Pastor"—simply a pastor who oversees about 50 groups) oversees 50 groups, 500 participants

L—Coordinator, oversees 5 groups, 50 participants

X—Small group leader, oversees 10 individuals

Xa—Small group apprentice leader

D

L   L   L   L   L   L   L   L   L

X   X   X   X   X

Xa

2. Modified meta design—The above model can be modified to fit your own situation. For example, the meta design may characterize a part of your small group ministry (i.e., "Covenant" groups). Perhaps recovery and support groups may fall under another type of oversight. Instead of staff pastors (D), you may require all staff to oversee five small groups, making your staff people "L's."

Example:

STAFF PERSON

Group   Group   Group   Group   Group

3. Multiple levels of ministry design—Highly structured program churches may offer various group types under existing church leadership. The Mission staff may oversee outreach/service teams; the pastoral staff the traditional covenant groups; the counseling staff may oversee the recovery and support groups.

Example:

CHURCH LEADERSHIP

Outreach   Discipleship   Pastoral Care   Assimilation

Evangelistic Groups   Recovery Groups

Covenant Groups   New Member Courses

4. Committee oversight design—All of the above models assume direct pastoral involvement. For some churches that may not be possible. In these types of churches an individual or a committee may handle oversight and training responsibilities. The above models may be modified by inserting "committee" wherever "staff" is written. One of the potential drawbacks of a committee structure, however, is that the details of responsibility can be overlooked.

5. Cell design—The cell church model is for small group purists. While the meta-church model may retain some of the distinctives of American church culture—such as a fellowship hour, Sunday school, and counseling ministry (to name a few)—the cell church uses small groups for *all* needs, including ministry to children and youth. An import from Third and Fourth World churches, the cell church includes two basic dimensions: one, celebrative worship; and two, all-encompassing, continuously multiplying groups.

6. *Scattershot design*—Finally, there is the Scattershot Design, or "Two Groups Going Nowhere." Although it is found in many churches (see chapter 2), it is not recommended.

Strategy Formulation Step 3
Complete Basic Small Group Information

For the next part of the strategy you will address certain specifics about small groups.

1. *How are small groups formed?* Most of the answers to this question are located in Strategy Formulation Step 1 (pp. 81-84). The fundamental issue underlying this question is: Whose responsibility is it to form groups? Some churches will give this responsibility to the staff; others to a computer. In my particular church, leaders are responsible for starting their own groups (I help by offering them names of potential members).

2. *How will group growth be handled?* In the meta and cell models, the answer is simple: An apprentice leader is trained and the group "births" a new group. If you do not employ a meta or cell model, you should still decide what to do with successful groups that, for instance, end up with twelve members. In order that groups may avoid becoming ingrown, group multiplication is recommended for larger groups.

3. *What size is appropriate?* Small group experts agree that groups function best with three to twelve individuals.

4. *How often must groups meet?* Some people may want to form a small group that meets monthly, or every several months. What direction will you give those groups?

5. *Where and when will groups meet?* In one sense, the answer to this question is very simple: anytime and anyplace. But the question raises group dynamic issues such as noise, lighting, space, and privacy.

6. *Open? Closed? Open/closed?* Small groups in many churches are closed. They are protective of their group life and selective of who may

join. Other churches, like cell and meta churches, require their groups to remain open and consistently inviting. My church encourages groups to close while in the midst of a study and to open at the beginning and end of the study (or covenant). It is a hybrid system that we call "open/closed."

7. *What kinds of groups will we allow?* There are several possibilities: discipleship (intensive spiritual growth); covenant (the majority of groups fit this category); recovery; support (mothers, widows, etc.); affinity (men's and women's groups, and so forth); Sunday school (run like small group); ministry/outreach; mission. If you do not allow certain group types, why not? How will you ensure that every group fits within the structure provided by the church for training and oversight?

8. *Other possible questions:* What happens during vacations (should we *require* groups to stop meeting in summer?)? How long are group meetings? What group studies and resources will be made available, and what resources are off limits?

By the time you complete this chapter, you will have provided the framework for small group ministry in your church. In the coming chapters you will continue to edit your work, trace ideas to their logical conclusions, and test your ideas against reality.

Questions to Answer

1. Design the ideal ministry:

a. *How will we ensure that small groups can help us reach out to FIRST-TIME VISITORS?*

b. *How will we ensure that small groups can help us produce ASSIMILATED MEMBERS?*

c. *How will we ensure that small groups can help us to bring healing to people in RECOVERY from abuse/addiction/ codependency?*

d. *How will we ensure that small groups can provide SUPPORT to those who need it?*

e. *How will we ensure that small groups can help us to MAKE DISCIPLES?*

f. *How will we ensure that small groups can help us to CREATE LEADERS in the church?*

g. *How will we ensure that small groups can help us in EVAN-GELISM/MISSION?*

2. *Structure the Ideal Ministry—Look over the basic small group structures within the chapter, and adapt/utilize/create a strategy that fits your unique situation. The structure should help you to understand several issues: a. how leaders will relate to each other from top down and bottom up; b. how successful groups may develop their own structure by birthing other groups; c. how the structure itself relates to the church leadership/hierarchy.*

To help you complete this task, it may be helpful to identify leaders, groups, ruling bodies, apprentice leaders, coordinators, and others, with short-hand designations (for example: Small group leaders = X; Coordinators of 10 small groups = Y).

Show your structure in the space below.

3. **Define basic information about small groups in your church.**
   a. *how will groups be formed?*
   b. *how will group growth be handled?*
   c. *what sizes are small groups?*
   d. *how often do/must groups meet to be considered a small group?*
   e. *where and when will groups meet (and, where can groups not meet?)?*
   f. *will groups be open? closed? open/closed?*
   g. *what kinds of groups will our church allow? encourage?*
   h. *what resources may groups use?*

CHAPTER 9

WHAT ARE OUR GOALS?

I did not keep a clean room when I was a child. My mother would periodically send me to my room, imprisoning me until I had cleaned it. Attempting to outwit my mother, I would move through the following stages:

Step 1: Slide everything under the bed and into the closet. This rarely, if ever, worked.
Step 2: Stuff everything into drawers, giving the room the appearance of being clean and straight. Sometimes this worked, but not often.
Step 3: Sit in the middle of the room and moan about how the job is too big and my resources too small: "My mother is so mean for expecting me to clean this mess!" This never worked—except to strengthen my mother's resolve.
Step 4: Grudgingly, clean the room (when my mother appeared willing to let me starve until I obeyed).

Through step four I discovered the secret of accomplishing big projects: Complete one small task at a time. If there were papers lying around, I would pull them together and go through them carefully. I attacked the toys by category, putting each in its appropriate place. Next, I sorted the dirty and clean clothes. From there I made the bed, emptied the trash, and dusted and vacuumed.

Many churches go through similar stages when they try to start small groups. They hear about small groups and the impact they can have on a church, so they immediately start a group. When this fails to significantly affect their church, as it often does, they move to step two: they clean up the process a little, perhaps even visiting a successful church and imitating its ministry. When this fails, they doom themselves to sit outside of the blessed circle of small group ministry churches (step three).

There is a fourth step to the process that some churches employ. They set goals and systematically address one issue at a time. Goal setting allows an individual or an organization to accomplish large dreams one task at a time. If purpose, vision, structure, and planning are the skeleton of change, then goal setting provides the muscle and flesh.

What Are Goals?

In the game of soccer, the goal is a target toward which all energy is directed. When the ball goes through the posts, a goal has been scored and success has been achieved.

In life and ministry, a goal (or objective) is a target or direction toward which energy is expended. In chapter 3, we observed the following about goals:

- A goal is made for each result that is important to success. You will create goals for each category and sub-category in your strategy.
- Each goal is to be specific and related to a single topic.
- A goal is measurable. It answers the question "Did we succeed?"
- A goal has a deadline attached. Some will be short, others intermediate, and still others long-term.
- A goal should challenge you to do things you have not done in a realistic manner.

Long-term Goals—Three to Eight Years

You can begin setting long-term goals by revisiting the strategy developed in chapters 8 and 9. A simple technique is to move the category and subcategory titles over to a separate page (see the end of this chapter for additional instructions), defining your ideals as goals. For example, I wrote the following under the heading "First-Time Visitor" in chapter 8:

First-Time Visitor. When a person enters a church for the first time, he will be insecure. Small groups can help visitors find a church home:

a. Every small group will use the "empty chair" activity. Small groups will include an empty chair in every meeting, and will pray for the Lord to spiritually prepare the person who is to sit in that chair.

b. Every small group will be "open" at significant times during the year, ready to invite newcomers into the group.

c. The pastor(s)/head of the follow-up committee will work closely with small group leaders to provide names of potential invitees.

d. In the entry or narthex of the church, there will be a noticeable and sharp visual display about small group ministry, with brochures and response forms available. In addition, small groups will maintain high profile through sermons, bulletins, and newsletters.

Here are your long-term goals for first-time visitors:

First-Time Visitor. Within the next five years, we will:

- Complete our small group strategy, including in it the empty chair idea and the open group concept.
- Create a small group leadership training course, incorporating the empty chair and open group into the course.
- Work with the pastoral staff to develop a system by which names of newcomers will be fed to appropriate group leaders for contact.
- Develop a complete marketing process so that small groups will have a highly visible place in our church (chapter 12).

Intermediate-term Goals: One to Three Years

Intermediate goals are one to three years in duration. Here are some sample intermediate goals:

Year Two of Plan:

- Create a small group leadership training course.
- Begin a small group newsletter for small group members.
- Place a well-designed bulletin board in the fellowship hall to advertise small group ministry.
- Run one leadership training group.
- Begin three new groups.
- Begin researching recovery groups so that we may begin one in year three.

Year Three of Plan:

- Run two leadership training groups.
- Begin six new groups.
- Begin a first recovery group, for addictions.
- Lead one complete worship service using skits, sermon, and testimonies to encourage members and friends to get involved in Christian discipleship.

Short-term Goals (Within One Year)

The most important goal setting involves the first year's goals. You may be tempted to do too much. Your targets need to be attainable, with a mild to moderate challenge. Here are some examples of short-term goals for the first year:

- Create and refine our church strategy (using this resource).
- Provide a complete copy of our strategy, and make a presentation of our goals and dreams to the church leadership.
- Begin a "pilot" group, testing the ideas in our strategy to make sure that they work.
- Prayerfully consider potential leaders within the church. Invite them to a meeting. We will show them our strategy and challenge them to consider participating in a leadership training course to be held early in the second year.
- Locate and/or create a leadership training resource.

If you begin one healthy group the first year, you may be surprised how quickly the ministry can grow to five in the second year; ten in the third; twenty in the fourth; and so on. However, if you start with ten in the first year, and they are not healthy, you may find they grow to twelve in the third; eight in the fourth; with enthusiasm dropping year after year.

Using Goals in Ministry

There are three disciplines that ensure you will not waste effort creating goals that are forgotten:

1. Evaluation. There may be structural items that need to be changed for the ministry to become more effective. Structural change has an impact on goals—so every change needs to be translated into revised goal setting. Evaluation is covered in greater depth in chapter 13.

2. Checkups. Next, you must regularly review goals you have set for a specific time period—making sure that you remain on track.

3. Adjustments. At some point(s) you may face circumstances and dynamics that render your goals unrealistic. You may then adjust the coming year's goals to reflect updated realities.

Steady As You Go

One step at a time—systematically, carefully, and in a disciplined manner—we can accomplish significant tasks for God. Allow your use of goals, carefully applied, to lead you into God's will for your church and its people.

Questions to Answer

1. Write down the five points that were made about goals early in the chapter:

a.

b.

c.

d.

e.

2. Long-term goals, to year _____. Go back to your strategy outline and write in the categories (i.e., "First-Time Visitor"; "Assimilating Member"). Then, make long-term goals for each:

3. Create intermediate goals through year _____, for each of the categories of your strategy.

4. Create one-year goals for year _____, for relevant categories of your strategy. (It is possible that one or more categories may be missed in the first year, to be built upon in the coming years.)

CHAPTER 10

WHO ARE OUR LEADERS?

E ntering my sophomore year in college, I felt called by God into ministry. I was studying for an accounting and business degree and had no prior ministry experience. When an opportunity for youth ministry at a local Methodist church presented itself, I took the job.

I was ill prepared for youth ministry. On my first evening, a fairly large group of young people came to "look me over." Although I was not battle tested, they were. Within the first half hour a twelve-year-old young lady sauntered in and cursed me out. Not a good confidence builder!

We played a game outside, then moved downstairs to get to know one another. I realized that I was in big trouble. I had never been in a healthy youth group. I had no idea what to do. Stalling them while I improvised a course of action, I employed the "Let's go around the room and get to know one another" trick. They were not overjoyed.

In the face of tough steel-town teens, I tried to be smooth. I attempted to look like I had my act together. In reality, I was a mess.

Then, God blessed me with an occurrence that changed the whole tone of the meeting and set the pace for my ministry. I have always chewed on pens as a nervous habit. On several occasions I have had unfortunate mishaps. None, however, had happened at a time like this.

The young people shared their names, which I recorded on a piece of paper. My hand was shaking. I inadvertently fell back into the bad habit of pen chewing. It exploded right in my mouth. While I tried to pretend nothing was wrong, blue ink began oozing out of my mouth and onto my shirt. The teens noticed, and sat up with interest. Then I said "Phooey!" "Phooey?" they asked one another. "What in the world is 'Phooey'?" We laughed hard together, and the ice was broken.

That event set in motion an adventurous two years together. God blessed us. And I learned a valuable lesson that first night: Effective leadership is first and foremost *real*.

What Is "Real"?

Modern culture creates images that are based on false perceptions. The media bombard us with constant information: from billboards, radio stations, newspapers and magazines, television, movies, the mail, and even the telephone. Each idea attempts to manipulate our perception of life. Marketing relies on creating voids that can only be filled with a certain product or life choice.

Words are cheap in our world. We no longer examine the logic and validity of ideas. Instead, we evaluate the source or speaker using criteria like charisma, presentation, and physical appearance.

Many churches have adapted to our media-driven world by speaking in culturally relevant terminology. A positive result is that we are learning to build bridges to our culture through our buildings, language, and manner. A negative result is that we uncritically assume the identity of perception creators. Stated another way, we become inauthentic.

This false culture poses serious problems when recruiting small group leaders. Small groups cannot survive on sweetness, happiness, and an "everything is okay" mentality. Relationships need to be rooted deeply in God's bountiful mercy and grace. You cannot go deep when everybody is trying to create and live in a world that is more fantasy than reality.

The central task of leadership development is not to choose flamboyant leaders who can impress, but steady shepherds who can guide. Groups need leaders who can see, live in, and speak about life as it really is, and make God a central part of their living and ministries.

Profile of an Effective Group Leader

When you look for small group leaders, do not necessarily turn to outspoken individuals who are great at teaching (that is, lecturing). Nor must you choose the most popular individuals in the church. I have discovered that quiet, nurturing individuals with a steady faith track record (or, in the case of new believers, a well-balanced life) make superior small group leaders. This type of person is generally teachable, humble, diligent, caring, honest, and real. Many churches pass over such individuals because they are not high profile leaders. They do not "toot their own horns," which is one reason to select them. People who make others look good are effective small group leaders.

In a spiritual gift profile they have strong service, giving, and pastoral gifts. They may also have administrative and leadership gifts, perhaps in a secondary role. They are the kinds of people who stay late after fellowship events to help clean up. Or they shovel snow off the sidewalk when nobody is around. They do not want or need accolades. They simply enjoy serving.

Selecting Leaders

Your plan from chapter 8 includes clues about how to locate leaders. For instance, if you choose the apprentice model, then each leader will be responsible for finding and training a potential leader from within their group. Apprenticing is perhaps the most foolproof method for choosing leaders. Apprenticed leaders can be nurtured slowly and tested in the context of an actual small group experience.

Here are several ways to locate leaders: First, within a small group (apprentice); second, by inviting promising individuals to small group leadership training; third, by allowing people to sign up and take small group leadership training at their own initiative; fourth, by encouraging staff to lead small groups.

When selecting leaders, prayer is the highest priority. Jesus prayed all night before selecting the twelve men who formed his inner circle of disciples.

Layers of Leadership

Further development of a leadership model involves "layering" leaders, creating integrated yet diverse leadership positions. You began developing a layer of leadership model in chapter 8, perhaps without even realizing it. An example from the meta model is: There are *apprentices; leaders* (who lead groups of 10); *coordinators* (who oversee 5 groups); and *district pastors* (who oversee 50 groups, 500 people).

Several questions address issues related to layering: First, what are the different leadership positions in the ministry (i.e., apprentice, leader, coordinator, committee member)? Second, at what point will certain layers be developed? (For example, most churches starting a ministry will not have a district pastor.) Third, what basic responsibilities come with each position?

At my current church we began with small group leaders, then added the apprentice layer. As small groups progressed, we began moving successful leaders (who had birthed at least two groups) into coordinator positions (overseeing five groups). As our church continues to grow, we will add staff to oversee larger networks of small groups.

Training Leaders

Small group leadership is probably the most demanding ministry job within the church context. Small group leaders "pastor" as many as ten people. When a member is in the hospital, the small group leader will visit. When someone is in emotional crisis, the leader will call and care. When the group is going through difficulties, the leader will lie awake at night—sometimes praying, sometimes crying, not always sure what to do.

Because of the difficulty of the position, leaders need training and support. Here are a few ways to equip leaders:

1. Pastor's discipleship/pilot group. In some churches, a pastor-led group meets for one year. When the year has ended, the pastor encourages the group to disband and begin several groups. The original group may decide to continue meeting once per month.

2. Self-study. Some people reading this book will be lay persons without pastoral support. Lay people can prepare themselves to start groups, perhaps by reading a training manual for leaders.

3. Weekend event. Some churches will use a Saturday, Friday-Saturday, or Friday-Sunday retreat time as a training event. Leadership basics can be stressed, with monthly training sessions that follow.

4. Training in brief. The *Big Book on Small Groups* has a format that allows the first four chapters to be used as an abbreviated training course. Serendipity groups have a basic training course that is six weeks in length. Brief training sessions are most effective in churches that have mature Christian leaders ready to lead, or an existing small group ministry.

5. Apprenticing. This model has been discussed at length already, but there are variations that can be created using the apprentice model. For instance, an apprentice can be required to go through formal small group leader training before leading his own group.

6. Leadership training course. Many churches require eight, ten, twelve, or even more weeks of intentional training.

7. Incubated groups. This model works well in tandem with a leadership training course. Instead of training individuals, groups (at least three individuals, and no more than six) can be invited to go through small group leader training together. When the course is completed, the group is already fully functional.

Training Materials

The next decision is what material to use for training. The appendix includes several leadership training materials that are available. An important consideration here is how you intend to inform leaders about your church's strategy for small groups (more on this in chapter 11).

Leadership Expectations

Another aspect of training and deploying leaders involves communicating what you expect of them. On pages 37 and 38 of *Using the Bible in Groups* (Westminster Press, 1983), Roberta Hestenes identifies four tasks of leaders:

Task 1—Pray. To seek God's will and direction in everything.

Task 2—Prepare. Every part of group life, including location, atmosphere, meeting time, and study.

Task 3—Guide. The group time, sensitively and clearly.

Task 4—Care. Especially when the group is not meeting and the real work of Christian love begins.

There are other things that are not a part of Hestenes' list. For instance, how will you connect the leader and group to the church? You might consider making monthly reports a requirement. You can also expect leaders to attend regular (monthly?) leadership support and training meetings. In addition, some churches make regular worship attendance a necessity for leaders.

Resourcing Leaders

Many churches offer resources for their leaders. Here are some suggestions:

1. Resources that feed leaders. Your church may purchase a subscription to a positive tool, such as *Discipleship Journal* by NavPress, for each small group leader. Web sites on the Internet such as the "Small Group Network" offer a monthly newsletter, a library of resources, and an online bookstore (i.e., http://smallgroups.com). These resources help to keep the leader up to date on issues related to faith development, small group ministry, and Christianity.

2. Resources for groups. Many churches develop a resource library of samples from as many different small group publishers as possible. A leader can review the resources and then share several choices with her group.

3. Resources to help leaders. A final resource alternative is material that helps leaders lead more effectively. Several youth ministry game books offer ideas for community building. Bible dictionaries, concordances, maps, and commentaries, if placed in an accessible location, can illumine difficult scripture texts.

Ongoing Supervision/Training

In some small group churches, leaders meet together as often as every other week. In other churches it may be once per month. Ongoing meetings are one example of the way that churches provide support and training to leaders.

What happens at the meetings? At my church we use a simple formula. First, we share what is happening in our groups (usually in groups of four). We listen to our various leadership situations, offering solutions to difficult group and individual problems. Second, we address the corporate church and begin laying the groundwork for future events (for example, a small group evangelism event). And third, we learn new skills by exploring group dynamic issues or by delving deeper into such functions as prayer, Bible study, worship, evangelism, and mission.

Some churches offer further training events, perhaps in a retreat format. Others bring in an outside speaker to enhance leadership skills.

Priesthood of Believers

In Reformed theology, the idea of the "priesthood of all believers" has been a central tenet of faith. However, although it is a central *belief,* it has rarely been a central *fact.* In reality, the church of Jesus Christ has primarily been a spectator sport since about the third century A.D. (with the advent of church buildings and "professional" church serv- ices).

There is nothing more radical (the word "radical" comes from the word "radix," which means "returning to the roots") than taking seri- ously the priesthood of all believers. We must give responsibility *to* the body of Christ *for* the body. This is best accomplished by giving pastoral responsibility to trained, supported, and motivated small group lead- ers.

By training small group leaders, you will be intentionally creating an army of people who can think, pray, and serve. By their sheer numbers, they will be able to do far more than one pastor or a pastoral staff. The ramifications are endless, the joy boundless, and the challenges limit- less.

Questions to Answer

1. What do you look for in potential leaders (gifts, personality, faith commitment, maturity, relationship to the church/family)?

2. What methods will your church use to recruit/discover leaders?

3. What is your training model for leaders? apprentices? coordinators? others?

4. What is your job description for potential leaders? apprentices? coordinators? others?

5. What ongoing requirements must leaders meet? apprentices? coordinators? others?

CHAPTER 11

HOW CAN WE CODIFY OUR STRATEGY?

W hen I was in seminary I performed an independent church growth study for a church. My study led me through board minutes, congregational meetings, several years of statistics, and surveys with church leaders. In a dusty file I found the by-laws and a mission design for the church. I quickly discovered what happens when these items are placed in a file cabinet. They are put aside, ignored, and then forgotten. Any direction they offered became irrelevant.

Many churches have invested in self-studies and consultations, only to put the results away—perhaps more from ignorance than rebellion. Change is difficult. Risk is scary. It is much easier to continue living as we have for generations.

Those who have invested time and energy planning do not want their efforts to be wasted, so let's discuss how to implement your strategy.

The Plan Takes Shape

To finish and implement your plan, follow these steps.

1. Complete the outline presented at the end of this chapter. You have been answering these questions all along. However, some may need to be put in narrative form and others edited a bit. A computer desktop

publishing program is helpful if it is available. You may adapt the basic index that is provided so that all work is tailored to your situation.

2. Compare your plan with the Appendix and make changes. The document in the appendix is the completed work from a church that followed the same steps found in this resource.

3. Make high quality copies available, and give a copy to each of your small group leaders. If the strategy is not made available, it will be forgotten.

How Will We Use It?

There are several ways to use your work. First, you can teach the strategy as part of your small group leader training. In our church we give a fun group quiz on the last day of training to test our leaders' comprehension of the plan.

Second, produce copies and make them available upon request to prospective members and small group members. Groups will become stronger the better informed your members are.

Third, you may make your plan available to other churches so that they can be encouraged to develop a plan of their own. Through networking in your community and/or denomination, you may influence your region in a positive way by helping other churches grow stronger.

Finally, pastors moving to a new church can share the plan with leaders at the new church. If you are a church that has lost its pastor, you can make implementation of your strategy part of your pastoral terms of call.

Blueprint for Growth

Congratulations! You have developed a growth blueprint for your church. Now, consult your design, sell it, work it, and persistently build it. Make adjustments as necessary, and solicit feedback from leaders, participants, and outsiders.

By God's grace, and as you continue to learn and grow, "Two Groups Going Nowhere" will become "Two Groups Going Somewhere," then "Multiplying Leaders and Groups," and finally "Multiplying Churches." God can do such things!

Questions to Answer

In this session, put together your final strategy statement. You can choose to complete the statement in any way you wish. The question numbers refer to questions at the end of each chapter. The following is a suggested outline, complete with page numbers, which can be adapted as necessary. Consult the appendix for additional ideas.

Page No.

1 Cover Page ("Small Group Handbook for _____ Church" with graphics)

2 Index—Table of Contents

Part I

3 Cover Page—"Part I — _____ Church Strategy"

4 Narrative—Who we are, and our small group history (refer to p. 28, Question 3; and p. 54, Question 4)

5 Narrative—Why small groups are important to our church (refer to p. 28, Question 2)

Part II

6 Cover Page—"Part II—Basics of Small Groups"

7-8 What we mean by small groups: definition, purpose, description of size, meeting frequency, and so forth. (refer to p. 29, Question 5; p. 77, Question 3; and p. 90, Question 3)

9 Values important to this small group ministry (refer to p. 70, Question 3)

Part III

10 Cover Page—"Part III—Our Vision"

11-12 Vision for small groups (refer to pp. 69-70, Question 1)

Part IV

13 Cover Page—"Our Strategy"

Starting Small Groups

Page No.

PART THREE
IMPLEMENTING THE PLAN

CHAPTER 12

How Will We Market and Recruit?

Until now the planning process has involved group design, leadership training, and church structure. It is time to consider how to fill small groups with the people they were designed to affect. Implementation of small group ministry requires marketing and recruiting. A positive marketing and recruiting strategy creates an environment in which people become excited to be involved in small groups.

Marketers attempt to match their product with potential clients. Since the product in this case is relationship oriented, marketing involves bringing people together in the context of a small group—creating a link between recruiting and marketing.

The plan you developed in the previous chapters already includes marketing and recruiting elements. The comprehensive outline provided in this chapter will fill in some of the blanks and provide you with a more thorough plan.

Setting Up the Program

Marketing and recruiting superimpose themselves over much of the strategy you have devised. They are the tools by which you begin to implement small groups in your congregation. Because their work is critical, your first concern is to build a leadership structure that assigns responsibility and guarantees follow-through. The structure may involve the church staff, a committee that oversees the ministry, or a person chosen specifically for recruiting and marketing.

There are several points to keep in mind when creating a leadership structure for marketing and recruiting:

1. Marketing and recruiting people concern themselves with multiple relationships and possibilities (discussed in the rest of the chapter). These two areas require significant leadership with varied responsibility.

2. The role of marketing and recruiting never ends. Small group ministry must always maintain a high profile within the congregation.

3. Person(s) working in the area of marketing need to understand the small group ministry *and* the people who are being targeted. This ensures sensitivity and relevance for the ministry.

Part I—Go Where the People Are

When a donut shop owner searches for a location, he attempts to discern the patterns and habits of the breakfast market. The owner wants the shop to be in the right place at the right time. Like the donut shop owner, small group marketing attempts to locate the ministry as "near" to targeted individuals as possible. There are many potential audiences: women, men, visitors, community, couples, recovering drug addicts, and others. Therefore, there are several means of reaching these people with small group possibilities.

1. Marketing through small groups. The best way to market the ministry is through small groups themselves. Word of mouth powerfully disseminates information.

To illustrate: Imagine the impact that would be felt if a family in your church won the Publisher's Clearing House Sweepstakes. People would notice even if the family attempted to maintain a low profile. The rumor mill would swing into action:

"What is happening with the Smith family?"

"You have noticed it, too?"

"Of course I have! You cannot help seeing the new cars, the nicer clothes. Did they receive an inheritance or something?"

"Well, I know, but they have asked me not to tell."

"Tell what?"

"Tell where they got the money."

"So, they got money from somewhere."

"I did not tell you that."

"Well, if they got it from somewhere, they either won it or received an inheritance."

"Again, you didn't hear it from me."

"They probably won a sweepstakes or lottery or something."

"How did you figure it out! I did not tell you!"

"But which lottery did they win?"

"It was not a lottery. It was a sweepstakes, and you have to promise not to tell anyone."

Many churches rue the existence of the rumor mill. Reputations can be destroyed, petty disagreements fanned, and little good done. But rumor mills also fulfill a positive purpose, especially for small group ministry. As more people get involved in small groups, change will occur and "inquiring minds will want to know": Why is that person so excited about her faith? Why do those people hug each other on Sunday? Why is that formerly miserable family sitting together and actually smiling?

Once the word gets out that lives are being changed, others will want to join the groups. Then, churches can recruit new members using several means:

a. Member recruitment. Whether doing evangelistic outreach or simply inviting an individual to join, the members of a group can help their groups to grow. One word of caution: Before inviting friends, the group has to decide *how* and *when* to bring in new members. For example, if a member wants to invite a friend, does the group first need to okay the invitation?

b. Offering testimonies. A pastor can encourage small group members to offer testimonies in newsletters or in worship. Testimonies offer evidence of God's power at work in our lives. They also provide a concrete demonstration of God working through small groups.

c. Targeting certain groups. You can train leaders to reach certain groups of individuals. I once led a training event that several widows attended. Later, we formed a group for widows, addressing a significant—and unknown—need within the church.

d. Trained leaders promote the ministry. Leaders have a direct investment in small groups. They want the ministry to succeed. As time goes by and the ministry matures, small group members and participants will move into leadership positions within the church. These people will then be in a unique position to promote the ministry.

You may be wondering, given the seeming informality of these ideas, how to encourage groups to promote themselves. Some of the ideas will occur naturally over time. Some will result from group design issues already addressed in your strategic plan. And some will happen because leaders are trained by the church to implement them—such as member recruitment and targeting of certain groups.

2. *Marketing through a follow-up program.* Carolyn entered our church the week after her mother's sudden death. Recently relocated to our area, she had wandered from God for a long time. In her hour of need she returned to the faith roots of her godly mother, and to her own dim memories of the church.

She received a warm welcome and a packet of information about our church. Then, in a call I placed to her the same week, she told me about her mother and shared some of her pain. I mentioned that several people in our church had also lost their parents and were dealing with similar grief. A few participated in a small group that met on Friday evening. Would she be interested?

She hesitantly agreed to try the group. The leader called her, and she joined the group. They rallied around her and understood her pain. Within a short period of time she became involved in the church.

This story illustrates how significant small groups can be in reaching newcomers. Newcomers possess many of the needs that draw individuals into groups: vulnerability; uncertainty; the necessity of making new friends; the desire to feel involved, wanted, and needed; and the willingness to take risks.

The following questions address the issue of targeting newcomers through marketing and recruiting. First, what brochures and other materials will be given to newcomers? How will they demonstrate the importance of small group ministry to your church? Second, in follow-up visits and calls, how can the idea of small groups be communicated so that newcomers consider groups a viable option? And third, how will individuals be funneled into groups—will they be given a choice; placed by a staff member; or screened through a survey?

3. *Marketing through new member courses.* Mark and Holly had been attending our church for ten months when they inquired about becoming members. Through our follow-up program we invited them to join a small

group, but they declined. They attended worship regularly, but were not deeply involved in the church.

They did, however, attend our eight week new member course. The course is designed to accomplish several things. First, members of the course participate in a small group. Our intent is to provide a positive experience so that new members will want a further taste of small group ministry. Second, the new member material guides new members to carefully examine their relationship with Jesus Christ. We want to ensure that they have made a commitment to Jesus Christ and are willing to grow in their faith. And third, members discover their spiritual gifts so that they may serve the church in ways that are appropriate to their maturity and abilities.

Mark and Holly participated in the new member course with six other individuals. They spent time during each meeting getting to know one another. The individuals began to bond and to share their Christian life together. At the end of the course, Mark and Holly invited the other new members to their home for a potluck meal and a time of fellowship. Because of their experience in the new member course, Mark and Holly signed up for our small group leader training course.

Some churches fear that they will scare potential members away by requiring anything of them. In fact, *not* requiring anything can lead to significant membership problems—high membership rolls and very low involvement. Small group style new member courses communicate membership responsibilities in a nonthreatening and relational manner.

Designing a new member course as a small group experience requires addressing several questions. First, how will the course be an actual small group experience? Second, how will the course or membership packet materials spell out the possibilities of, importance of, and means of joining small groups? Third, how will people be matched with the best possible group upon completion of the course? And fourth, who will lead the new member groups?

The best way to draw new members into small groups is to recruit trained leaders to lead the course. The new member course can become a small group if all or several of the participants are willing.

Part II—Put the Ministry in Front of the People

Imagine standing in front of a grocery shelf loaded with boxes of soap and detergent. Your purpose is to locate the right floor cleaner. How will you decide which is best for your situation? Marketers know that the brands with the highest profile will be the ones most likely chosen. "Name recognition" is important to those looking for items to purchase.

The name recognition phase of marketing involves keeping the idea of small groups constantly in people's minds. For example, a well placed bulletin board, tastefully done, can create a positive image of the ministry.

Not all traditional methods of marketing and recruiting are necessary or acceptable in the church. Marketing should be done in good taste, without undue pressure or manipulation. Emphasize positive ideas (what groups can do) rather than the negative (don't you care about your faith?).

There are a number of ways to communicate the benefits of small groups to the church. Here are a few of the many possibilities:

- Bulletin boards
- Newsletter articles, advertisements
- Special banquets
- Church bulletins
- Follow-up and new member packets
- Needs surveys
- Multimedia through worship, radio, TV
- Worship service skits, special services, testimonies, sermon series
- Direct mail
- An annual "Small Group Membership Push" (late summer/fall)
- Computer matching services, where people fill out a questionnaire listing their best times for meeting, their needs, and so on, and they are placed in a group.

Consider which of these ideas will be viewed negatively by the potential audience. Next, identify those ideas that will be viewed most positively by the same audience. Set the negative ideas aside, and implement the positive ones.

Slick Salesmanship

When you market and recruit for small groups, you can take comfort in the fact that you are selling a product that is life changing (and free!). If you start with honesty, and mix in some real-life testimonies, your marketing will not be manipulation, but invitation. People will respond to Jesus' "follow me" call much more readily.

Questions to Answer

1. What marketing and recruiting issues and categories already exist in your strategy?

2. What leadership structure is/will be in place to ensure that marketing and recruiting occur?

    a. Who are the leaders/how will they be chosen?

    b. What will be their job description and accountability?

Marketing and Recruiting, Part I—Go Where the People Are

3. Small Group Recruitment:

    a. How will we encourage groups to recruit members?

    b. At what times will they be encouraged to recruit?

    c. What training, if necessary, will they be given?

4. What other means will be used to encourage groups and leaders to market for themselves? (i.e., testimonies by group members, targeting certain kinds of people in the church for their groups, placing trained leaders on different boards of the church for exposure)

5. How will we market and recruit through visitor follow-up?

    a. Promotion materials in follow-up packs?
    b. Follow-up calls stressing small groups? Who? How? Special
       training?
    c. Screening and placement for potential new members?

6. How will we market and recruit through new member courses?

    a. new member course designed like small group?
    b. new member course materials emphasize small groups?

c. new members encouraged to join/form small groups, and how?

Marketing and Recruiting, Part II—Put the Ministry in Front of the People

7. Which of the following methods will we use for putting small groups continually before the people?

  a. bulletin boards
  b. newsletter articles, advertisements (when? how?)
  c. special banquets
  d. church bulletins
  e. follow-up and new member packets
  f. needs surveys
  g. multimedia (slides, videos, skits, etc.) through worship, radio, TV
  h. worship service kits, special services, testimonies, sermon series
  i. direct mail
  j. special "group membership push" in late summer, fall (or other time)
  k. computer/staff matching (people fill out questionnaires and are matched with appropriate groups)
  l. other:

8. Review the results of your work in this session, and:

  a. Add to your short, intermediate, and long-term goals as necessary.
  b. Refine your work so that it is understandable and workable.
  c. Condense your work from this session and give to appropriate staff, committees, leaders.

CHAPTER 13

How Will We Evaluate and Make Adjustments?

I n the previous chapters of this resource you have given prayerful attention to hundreds of small group issues. The strategy you have developed is the foundation, or launching pad, of the ministry. The same care you have given to the birth and infancy of the ministry must now be employed to carry it through to maturity. Evaluation allows you to monitor progress as the ministry grows.

We evaluate to ensure quality. Misguided leaders and negative group behavior will damage the entire small group ministry. Evaluation allows you to correct mistakes and strengthen every facet of ministry.

We also evaluate to promote an atmosphere of accountability. Small group leaders are volunteers. Some churches may be tempted to pamper leaders and to make their choices easy. Accountability demands high standards and encourages effective leadership support.

Evaluation does not often occur naturally. We dislike constantly checking ourselves, our motives, and our results.

An intentional leadership structure creates the environment in which evaluation will occur. The leadership structure might be small group leaders, a committee that oversees the ministry, or staff/coordinators. The possibility of ongoing evaluation is strengthened when you use an existing leadership structure.

Developing an Evaluation Cycle

Effective evaluation follows the rhythm and life of small groups. Developing a yearly cycle makes evaluation appear natural—for example, by requiring leaders to file monthly or quarterly evaluations. Instead of feeling that somebody is looking over their shoulders, leaders involved in healthy evaluation process sense that their support system for the ministry provides a foundation and a measure of necessary control. There are several questions that provide the basis for evaluation.

1. What is our timetable for gathering information and evaluating? Leaders may be given a worksheet or report to fill out after each of their small group meetings. Or, they may submit a report to their supervisor once a month. These forms can help the leader and/or supervisor perceive a group's strengths and weaknesses. Monthly leadership meetings could include time for self-evaluation. Some churches may also choose more infrequent times, like once a quarter or year, to offer questionnaires and more formal evaluation tools for groups and leaders.

2. What are the criteria for evaluation? Part of the answer to this question is already included in your strategy (if you followed the format outlined in chapter 11, this will cover pages 18-21 of your small groups strategy manual, including Leadership, Group Life/Growth/Assimilation/New Member/Recruitment, and Evangelism/Mission). At least once a year evaluate to determine what progress is being made in each of the important areas of ministry.

A second potential evaluation source are the short, long, and intermediate goals that you set. You can evaluate your progress every six months and adapt the goals to your current realities.

A third source is that of small group leaders themselves. Good questions allow leaders to evaluate themselves, their groups, and the overall ministry, for effectiveness and potential weaknesses. If leaders have a job description, use the categories included in the job description to evaluate them.

3. What methods shall we use to gather information and evaluate? Some of the possibilities include surveys, one-on-one meetings, small group and leadership meetings, and weekly/monthly forms that leaders complete.

4. How shall we institute the changes necessary to bring the ministry to the next level? Information processed through evaluation will bring into focus changes that may be necessary. (If only one group member or leader complains, the system may not need to be changed. Solicit feedback from staff, leaders, and group members to determine whether systemic change is necessary.) If you make a structural change, then the ministry strategy needs to be adjusted and new goals created. Remember to communicate these changes to the group leaders.

A few years ago I sifted through year-end small group leader evaluations. After reading through the reports, I was convinced that several things needed adjustment. A number of the small groups felt little sense of direction. The groups felt no connection to the church. Some were growing stale. Several leaders were not being fed or directed.

While still processing the information, I moved to a new church. In my new setting, I listed the negatives and positives of my previous small group situation. I developed a plan that has evolved into this book. I was open to evaluation and to new ideas in order to improve my leadership.

Good-Better-Best

The first small group I started was a transformational experience for me, and life-changing for those involved. I observed with enthusiasm and joy the group submitting itself to the claims of Jesus Christ. Looking back on that experience provides me with happiness and nostalgia.

I also look back on that experience as the beginning of a pilgrimage in learning *how* to make disciples. The first group was good, but not good enough. I missed many cues as a leader. We did not address several important issues. We had a limited self-understanding.

Through the process of evaluation, I began to uncover ideas that have better equipped me to lead. The process of evaluating and making changes now continues each year, in each setting and situation in which I find myself.

Heaven will be the ultimate small group experience. Until that day, you and I must continue to pray, learn, weep, laugh, struggle, and grow, to the end that in this life we receive a taste of the love of God, in community.

Questions to Answer

1. What is our leadership structure for evaluation, and what accountability will ensure that evaluation occurs?

2. What is our timetable for evaluation?

    a. Regular evaluation? when/how?

    b. Infrequent evaluation? when/how?

3. What criteria will be used for each of the above timetables, and who will provide the information in each case?

4. What methods shall we use to gather the information desired?

5. How will we examine the information and make changes?

    a. Who will examine and make changes?

    b. What will be required of people examining information and making changes? (remember to adjust strategy and goals when changes are made)

    c. How will changes be communicated to leaders and groups?

APPENDIX

A SAMPLE CHURCH STRATEGY

First Church
Small Group Leader's Handbook

Table of Contents

The church profiled in this appendix is an actual church that completed the planning process detailed in this book. Although the name of the church has been changed to "First Church," except for some editing, the material is unchanged.

First Church is a church from a mainline denomination, located in a middle-class area of the inner city. It possesses ethnic, suburban, and inner-city elements, and is beginning to grow after years of stagnation. The material that follows is their Small Group Leader Handbook.

Appendix

Our Small Group History

The people of First Church believe that:

- God calls us to worship Him, publicly and privately, with our hearts, minds, and souls.
- God calls us to be firmly rooted in his word.
- God calls us, as individuals who have been redeemed by the blood of Jesus Christ and filled by the Holy Spirit, to draw others into God's kingdom and help them to grow in their Christian walk.

Our small group history began in the early 1980s with a pilot group that met with the pastor for several months. The group's intent was to introduce the idea of small groups to the church and to train potential leaders. Five groups formed from that initial small group experience.

In several ways the groups, which focused on fellowship, prayer, and Bible study, were successful. The people in the groups nurtured and encouraged one another. Different ages, races, and nationalities were integrated through group involvement. At the time that the ministry began, First Church included a large group of Hmong people; many were new Christians, and at least ten became regular participants in small groups.

There were also negative aspects of our small group ministry. The groups did not have clearly defined goals, and there was little communication with the pastor or Spiritual Life Committee. There was no ongoing training of leaders, little coordination among the various groups and the small group ministry coordinating team, and no accountability of each group to the church. Most groups disbanded after two years, although some continued meeting. Several groups have recently begun meeting on an ad hoc basis, without church supervision or support.

In November 1995, we are a church of 200 members with an average Sunday morning worship attendance of 205—up from 150 a year ago.

There are a number of new people attending and joining our church. At least half of those attending morning worship entered our church within the past two years. There is a Sunday evening Bible study that is attended by twenty-five to thirty individuals, and a Wednesday evening class that studies theology. A men's prayer meeting is held on Thursdays at 6:30 A.M. with eight men in attendance. Usually six to eight women attend the women's prayer meeting which is held on Tuesday mornings at 6:45 A.M.

Our Sunday school includes fifty to sixty children and adults each week. We offer two adult classes with ten members in each class. In addition, a new member class meets during the Sunday school hour for eight weeks, three times a year. For our children and youth we offer classes for Primaries, Juniors, and Senior High students. Due to a large number of preschool children in the congregation, an infant and toddler nursery is provided.

We have a Youth Group meeting each Sunday night that includes ten young people. A new children's outreach program, Kid's Club, meets for eight week sessions three times per year. Each Friday night, we host a dinner to feed the hungry that serves over one hundred people.

In addition to our two prayer meetings and Bible studies, there are seven active small groups meeting, four of which are ongoing and three which began recently.

Why We Do Small Group Ministry

We believe that God is calling First Church to experience community together in small groups; to bear witness to the Gospel in the world; to worship God and proclaim His Word; and to minister to those in need.

A small group is an intentional gathering of a small number of people who commit themselves to regular meetings for the purpose of becoming better disciples of Jesus Christ. Small groups are important to First Church because:

1. they are biblical.
2. they help us learn and practice Christian principles.
3. they help us build relationships.
4. they provide support.

5. they provide a forum to pray for one another.
6. they provide an opportunity for accountability.
7. they offer discipleship.
8. they offer opportunities for evangelism.
9. they offer opportunities for service within and outside of the group.

Small Group Basics

Definition: A small group is an intentional gathering of a small number of people who commit themselves to regular meetings for the purpose of becoming better disciples of Jesus Christ.

Mission Statement: Through the small group ministry at First Church, people will be reconciled to God and to one another.

Size: Each group will have between five and ten members, including one leader and one apprentice leader.

Meeting Frequency: Groups are encouraged to meet three times per month, or a minimum of two times per month. We encourage that two of the three meetings be for sharing, Bible study and prayer. The third meeting can be for service or socializing.

Administrative Structure: The administrative structure is a modified meta-church design: (1) Small groups of from five to ten individuals that include a leader and apprentice; (2) Coordinators who work with four to five group leaders; (3) and members of a Small Group Committee, including the pastor, associate pastor, and coordinators.

The coordinators will meet with assigned group leaders at least once during each month, to offer support and guidance. All of the leaders, apprentice leaders, coordinators, and pastors will meet monthly for mutual support, training, nurture, and worship. The Small Group Committee meeting will be held on the fourth week of the month.

Duration of a small group: When a group is formed, the leader and the group members will commit to a minimum group life of three months. Each group will create a covenant which will last for no more than six months. The covenant can be renewed at six-month increments (or less if desired). If a group grows to more than ten, the apprentice leader and several of the group members will birth a new group.

If a group continues meeting past a year, the group, together with its leader and coordinator, will evaluate whether the group should continue, birth a new group, disband, or find another mission.

Our Small Group Ministry Theology

1. The Bible reveals that the one true God exists in divine community (Father, Son, and Holy Spirit).
2. God created humankind in His image as community (Genesis 1:26-27 and Genesis 2:18).
3. Sin destroys relationships.
4. Scripture teaches us that God refuses to leave us alone in our self-destruction. God enters our world through Jesus Christ, calling us to come and be healed. Only God can create community and bring restoration to the brokenness we experience because of sin.
5. We are commanded by our Lord and Head of the Church, Jesus Christ, to make disciples of all the world. A disciple of Jesus Christ is a person who is committed to following Him in obedience to His word and who seeks to continually grow in intimate relationship with Him. Disciples are made in relationship. Following the example of our Lord, we will seek to make disciples through small groups.

Our Small Group Ministry Values

a. *God*—our small groups exist to worship and bring glory to God.

b. *Individuals*—the community of faith lived out in small groups will affirm individuals by: Holding them accountable for their growth; listening in a positive manner when they speak; and encouraging them to use their spiritual gifts.

c. *Reconciliation*—our small groups will use tools such as group covenants and honest sharing to provide the environment in which reconciliation can occur.

d. *Recovery*—our small groups will encourage people to admit their hurts and faults so that they may experience the healing touch of God in community.

e. *Support*—our small groups will help connect individuals to others experiencing similar stresses and pains.

f. *Visitors*—our small groups will be the means by which we welcome newcomers into the healing, forgiving family of faith.

g. *Discipleship*—through our small groups we will call individuals to respond in obedience to all that God requires.

h. *Community*—our small groups exist to build the deep relationships which will foster disciple-making.

i. *Leadership Development*—in our caring small group environment, leaders will be developed.

j. *Outreach*—our small groups will be the primary vehicle by which our church loves, serves, and evangelizes the world around us.

Vision Statement

We, at First Church, are committed to a strong, dynamic, small group ministry that significantly ministers to:

- Newcomers entering our church

- Those who need healing and support

- The overall church as we grow

- Our congregation in the areas of prayer, evangelism, disciple-making, worship, and mission

- Our community and the world as we train and mobilize leaders to make a difference for the glory of God.

Mission Statement

Through our small groups at First Church, individuals will experience reconciliation to God and to one another.

Small Group Leadership Strategy

Our leaders will be individuals with a steady faith track record who are: Willing; humble; diligent; caring; honest; authentic; and teachable.

Leaders will have some or all of the following spiritual gifts: Service; giving; administration; leadership; and pastoral care. Our small group leaders will be nurturers and pastors to their small groups. The leader is not a teacher but a facilitator.

Small group leadership training will be done in one of the following ways:

1. **Incubated groups.** Anyone interested in being a leader may form a small group consisting of four individuals. A coordinator will facilitate the group for four to six weeks. The coordinator will train the leader to lead the group by the end of the four to six weeks.

2. **Pastor's discipleship pilot group.** Our pastors will start groups (similar to incubated groups) that will meet together for four months. At the end of that time the groups will disband and form several other groups.

3. **Apprenticing.** Each group will have an apprentice leader who will learn from being in the group and working with the leader and the coordinator. Appropriate training and reading materials will be used for training.

4. **Training in brief.** An individual or group can meet with a coordinator over four sessions to study *The Big Book on Small Groups* and a videotape training series by Serendipity.

5. **Ongoing supervision and training.** The small group leaders and apprentices will meet monthly with the coordinators and pastors to: Share what is happening in our groups (in groups of three or four); learn new skills in prayer, study, worship, evangelism, mission, and group dynamics; talk about the church and plan events for small groups in the church; and develop our connection to the church.

Small Group Strategy

1. Newcomers and First Time Visitors

Newcomers and visitors will be contacted through the evangelism committee and the pastoral staff. The pastor or follow up chair will let the group leaders know of any newcomers who are interested in becoming a part of a small group. We will display our small group benefits on bulletin boards in the Narthex and Fellowship Hall. We will make brochures and a response form available. Ongoing small groups will be encouraged to invite new members. Small groups will include an empty chair at every meeting as members pray for the Lord to prepare the person who is to sit in that chair.

2. Christian/Assimilated Member

An assimilated member regularly attends worship, participates in the life of the church, gives regularly, and has at least six friends in the church. To assimilate newcomers into active participation in our church, we will:

a. Encourage potential new members to participate in our eight week new member course (small group style). We will limit the groups to about ten individuals, and they will meet on Sunday mornings or on a week night. The course will be led by the associate pastor, with potential group leaders joining during the last three meetings (in case the group wants to continue as a small group).

b. At the end of the new members class, persons wishing to join the church will be asked to become actively involved in First Church. They may continue as a small group with the other new members; join an existing small group; join the choir; attend Sunday school; or participate in other activities such as Kids' Club.

c. Those wishing to join First Church will meet with the pastor and elders. They will formally join the church if it is clear to the pastors and the potential member that they are clearly being led to join this body of Christ.

d. The new members class will be offered 3 times a year. Each course will include discussion on how to become a Christian, how we know we are a Christian, the role and discernment of spiritual gifts, and the place of small group ministry in Christian growth. Each new member class should be considered a recruiting ground for small groups.

e. Ongoing small groups who are open to accepting new members will be publicized so that new members of the church who wish to join may.

3. Recovery Groups

Many people in our city and our church have recovery issues related to physical or sexual abuse, grief and bereavement, separation or divorce, and alcohol or drug abuse. These issues may be all consuming to the people involved. Until people are able to work past pain, they tend to remain in the same place and are unable to grow spiritually. As appropriate to the current needs in our church and as trained leaders are available, we will offer recovery groups to assist people in healing their pain. At appropriate points in their recovery process, we will encourage recovery group members to become part of discipleship small groups.

4. Support Groups

There are many times in our lives when we find ourselves facing difficult times. In these times a friend in similar circumstances can make all the difference. Support groups can be a significant factor in people's lives during these times, as they place homogeneous groups like mothers, couples, widows or widowers, and pastors together to help deal with similar problems. As they are needed, support groups will be offered in areas where trained leaders are available. Marriage enrichment and parenting are areas where we could currently offer support groups. These groups would be encouraged to study an entire range of discipleship topics over a period of time so that they do not remain fixed on a specific type of circumstance. These groups could be offered to members of the church and to members of the community as a method of outreach.

5. Covenant Groups

The goal of every small group is to make disciples that reflect Jesus Christ in every aspect of their lives. Disciples are made in the community of two or more believers. Each group will begin by agreeing to a covenant, in conjunction with a small group coordinator. The covenant will include the commitment to make the group a priority, to attend regularly, to keep other members in prayer, and to be accountable one to another. The focus and passion of these small groups will be on relationship building, to the Lord and to one another. Over time, each group will grow by inviting newcomers, and when necessary will birth a new group. These groups may develop a service to the church or community which will evidence God's life changing love and our desire to share it. Every group will be encouraged to pray for specific friends, relatives, or neighbors, as in the Masters Plan Program.

6. Mission Involvement with Groups

We define mission as when a person serves others locally, nationally, or internationally. Some groups may wish to become directly involved in local mission projects and will become service groups. Other groups may decide to participate in such projects sporadically. Some groups may directly support missionaries or go on short-term mission trips. All groups will be encouraged to participate in a mission activity at some level, no matter how small.

Objectives

One Year Goals

1. Train four people who are not currently involved in small groups in a 3 month leadership training course. The intent is to start 2-4 new small groups with these people as leaders.

2. Begin ongoing supervision and training meetings for small group leaders and apprentices, with the nurture team and pastors, that meet monthly.

3. Develop and print a brochure with information on small groups, and a registration form.

4. Begin three new small groups within six months.

5. To have one hundred people involved in small groups within one year.

Three Year Goals

1. To have thirty small group leaders trained.
2. To have two hundred people involved in small groups.
3. To have every small group member involved.

Apprentice/Co-Leader Job Description

Assignment: To assist the group leader in leading, facilitating, and equipping the members of a group so that together they will fulfill their group mission.

Qualification:

1. Member of our church, or active non-member.
2. Person with desire to exercise his/her spiritual gifts.
3. One who shares and believes in the vision of the church to disciple others through small group ministry.

4. One who is teachable.

5. One who has an ability to communicate well with others.

6. One who possesses spiritual maturity as assessed by the pastoral staff.

Responsibilities:

1. Recruit a host/hostess to see that child care, refreshments, and appropriate seating for the group is available.

2. Follow up with all prospects and members through personal visits, phone calls, and correspondence.

3. Set out an open chair for each meeting as a constant reminder to the group of the need for new participants and new conversion growth.

4. Maintain unity, agreeing not to teach or practice those things which are contrary to the teachings of the church.

5. Accept responsibility for developing relationships with (and extending invitations to) the group, and to unchurched, and unbelieving people.

6. Submit a monthly report to the coordinator for your group.

7. Birth a new group when sufficient growth occurs.

8. Pray for each member and prepare for each meeting.

9. Notify pastoral staff of acute crisis conditions requiring response.

Reporting Relationships:

1. The apprentice reports to the group leader.

Training and Development:

1. Orientation 4-6 sessions.

2. Monthly ongoing training with the other leaders.

3. Take advantage of the training opportunities as they become available.

Host/Hostess Job Description

Assignment: To assist the group leader and his/her apprentice by providing a home or comfortable place for the meeting.

Qualifications:

1. Member of our church or regular church attendance.

2. Person with desire to exercise his/her spiritual gifts.

3. One who shares and believes in the vision of the church to disciple others through small group ministry.

4. One who is teachable.

5. One who has an ability and willingness to communicate well with others.

Responsibilities:

1. Provide a home (or a comfortable meeting place), and arrange chairs in conjunction with the leader. (A circle is preferred.)

2. Set up the simple refreshments before the meeting time in order to be ready to greet the guests and regular attenders.

3. Have extra Bibles, paper, and pens for those who forget theirs.

4. Have a genuine interest in each guest and greet them at the door with a warm smile.

5. Set the atmosphere of love and acceptance for everyone, calling them by their first names and introducing guests to others.

6. Wait until guests have left before cleaning up and rearranging furniture.

Reporting Relationships:

1. The host/hostess reports directly to the group leader.

Small Group Leader/Apprentice Application

Please answer each question as completely as you can. (You will be interviewed by the Associate Pastor based on this confidential application, and you will receive a copy of it. Thank you for your interest and truthfulness.)

Name

Address

Date of Birth _____ Male_____ Female_____

Personal Background

1. How long have you lived in this area?

2. Do you work outside your home? Yes___ No___

3. Marital Status: Married___ Single___ Divorced___ Separated___ Widowed___

4. Names and grade levels of any children.

5. How long have you been attending First Church?

6. Are you a member of First Church? Yes___ No___. If so, for how long? ___ years.

7. Why did you choose First Church as your church of membership?

8. What activities have you been involved in since attending First Church?

Spiritual Background

1. How long have you been an active, worshiping member of the Christian church?

2. Give a brief description of what Jesus means to you.

3. What portion of the day do you spend in prayer and Bible study?

4. A God-given strength of my Christian walk is:

5. A barrier to overcome in my Christian walk is:

Past Involvement Small Group Ministry

1. I have participated in small group meetings. Yes___ No___

2. In those groups I was a: member___ leader___ apprentice___ host___ other___.

3. Briefly describe your feelings about that experience:

Current Interest in Small Groups

1. I believe the primary purpose of small groups at First Church is:

2. I want to be involved with small groups because:

3. My greatest leadership strength is:

4. My greatest fear in leadership is:

5. If you are married, does your spouse support you in this leadership position? Yes___ No___

6. Your small group leadership interest is: Leader___ Apprentice Leader___ Host___

Doctrinal Statement

1. I believe that I am by nature sinful and need God's grace for the forgiveness of my sins. Yes___ No___

2. I believe that Jesus Christ, God's son, gave himself for the forgiveness of my sins on the cross of Calvary.   Yes___ No___

3. I believe that I have eternal life as a free gift by grace through faith in Jesus Christ. Yes___ No___

4. I believe that the Bible is God's Word and is the only divine rule and standard for my Christian faith and life. Yes___ No___

5. I accept the teachings of First Church as summarized in the book of order. Yes___ No___

6. I believe in the Triune God, Father, Son, and Holy Spirit. Yes___ No___

Small Group Leader's Monthly Report

Leader's Name _____

Month _____   Number of Meetings _____

Group Name _____Current Covenant Ends _____

Please Rate the Group from 1 to 5 (1 being "needs improvement," 5 being "terrific")_____

Members' Names:

Using the letters: R = Community Building, S = Study, Worship, and Prayer, and O = Outreach, make a circle in the space below dividing it into three sections demonstrating the way your group looks:

What is your group currently studying?

What worries you about the group?

What brings you joy?

How is your group growing?

1. In love for each other?

2. In love for God?

3. In desire to reach out to others?

Small Group Covenant

This covenant runs from _____ until _____.*

Who we are:

Type of Group

Group Members (special criteria for membership? Names of current members):

Attendance expectations:

When and how we accept new members:

Communication Ground Rules (honesty? gossip? affirmation? and so on).

What we do:

Meeting Time/Place/Frequency:

Meeting activities (which of the following we will do, and how much time is spent doing each?):

- Community Building
- Study
- Worship
- Evangelism
- Mission/Outreach

Schedule of Events in a typical evening/meeting:

---

*Note: Covenants should not run for longer than six months.

Notes

1. Small Group Basics

1. Robert Wuthnow, *Sharing the Journey* (New York: Free Press), 1994.
2. Leith Anderson, *Dying for Change* (Minneapolis: Bethany House Publishers, 1990), chapter 2, pp. 26-41.
3. Ibid., p. 30.
4. Gareth Icenogle, *Biblical Foundations for Small Group Ministry* (Downers Grove, Ill.: InterVarsity Press, 1994).
5. Jeffrey Arnold, *The Big Book on Small Groups* (Downers Grove, Ill.: InterVarsity Press, 1991), p. 9.
6. M. Scott Peck, *The Different Drum: Community Making and Peace* (New York: Simon and Schuster, 1987), pp. 59-76.
7. Carl George, *The Coming Church Revolution* (Grand Rapids: Fleming H. Revell, 1994), pp. 62-74.

3. What Is Strategic Planning?

1. Arthur A. Thompson and A. J. Strickland III, *Strategy Formulation and Implementation* (Boston: BP/Irwin, 1980), p. 5.

5. What Do We Value?

1. Gareth Icenogle, *Biblical Foundations for Small Group Ministry*, p. 27.
2. Leith Anderson, *A Church for the 21st Century* (Minneapolis: Bethany House Publishers, 1992), p. 128.

Notes

6. What Do We Want to Value?

1. Leith Anderson, *A Church for the 21st Century* (Minneapolis: Bethany House, 1992), pp. 103-8.

7. What Is Our Purpose?

1. C. S. Lewis, *The Great Divorce* (New York: Macmillan, 1946), pp. 8-9.

BIBLIOGRAPHY

Anderson, Leith. *A Church for the 21st Century* (1990) and *Dying for Change* (1992). Minneapolis: Bethany House Publishers.

Arnold, Jeffrey. *The Big Book on Small Groups, Discovering the Bible for Yourself* (1993), and *Small Group Starter Kit* (1995). Downers Grove, Ill.: InterVarsity Press.

Bunch, Cindy. *Small Group Idea Book: Resources to Enrich Community, Worship and Prayer, Nature and Outreach.* Downers Grove, Ill.: InterVarsity Press, 1996.

Coleman, Robert. *The Master Plan of Evangelism.* Old Tappan, N.J.: Fleming H. Revell Co, 1963.

Corrigan, Thom. *The Small Group Fitness Kit.* Colorado Springs, Colo.: NavPress/Pilgrimage Publishing, 1996.

Easum, William. *Dancing with Dinosaurs: Ministry in a Hostile and Hurting World.* Nashville: Abingdon Press, 1993.

Elms, LeRoy. *Disciples in Action.* Colorado Springs, Colo.: NavPress, 1981.

George, Carl. *Prepare Your Church for the Future* (1991) and *The Coming Church Revolution: Empowering Leaders for the Future* (1994). Grand Rapids, Mich.: Fleming H. Revell.

Hardaway, Wright and DuBose. *Home Cell Groups and House Churches: Emerging Alternatives for the Urban Church.* Nashville: Broadman Press, 1987.

Bibliography

Hestenes, Roberta. *Using the Bible in Groups* (1985) and *Turning Committees Into Communities* (1991). Philadelphia: Westminster Press.

Icenogle, Gareth. *Biblical Foundations for Small Group Ministry*. Downers Grove, Ill.: InterVarsity Press, 1994.

Jacks, Bob, et al. *Your Home, a Lighthouse*. Colorado Springs, Colo.: NavPress, 1986; rev. ed., 1987.

Long, Jimmy (coordinator). *Small Group Leaders' Handbook*. Downers Grove, Ill.: InterVarsity Press, 1995.

McBride, Neal. *How to Build a Small-Group Ministry* (1996) and *How to Lead Small Groups* (1995). Colorado Springs: NavPress.

Mack, Michael. *The Synergy Church: A Strategy for Integrating Small Groups and Sunday School*. Grand Rapids, Mich.: Baker Books, 1996.

Mulholland, Jr., Robert. *Invitation to a Journey*. Downers Grove, Ill.: InterVarsity Press, 1993.

Neighbour, Jr., Ralph. *Where Do We Go from Here? A Guidebook for the Cell Group Church*. Houston: Touch Publications, 1990.

Ott, E. Stanley. *The Joy of Discipling and the Vibrant Church*. Grand Rapids, Mich.: Lamplighter Books, 1989.

Peace, Richard. *Small Group Evangelism*. Downers Grove, Ill.: InterVarsity Press, 1985.

Peck, M. Scott. *The Different Drum: Community Making and Peace*. New York: Simon and Schuster, 1987.

Stedman, Ray. *Body Life*. Ventura, Calif.: Regal Books, 1972.

Steele, Les. *On the Way: A Practical Theology of Christian Formation*. Grand Rapids, Mich.: Baker Books, 1990.

Warren, Rich. *The Purpose Driven Church: Growth Without Compromising Your Message and Mission*. Grand Rapids, Mich.: Zondervan Publishing House, 1995.

Williams, Dan. *Seven Myths About Small Groups*. Downers Grove, Ill.: InterVarsity Press, 1991.

Wuthnow, Robert. *Sharing the Journey* (1996) and *"I Came Away Stronger": How Small Groups Are Shaping American Religion* (1994). New York: Free Press.